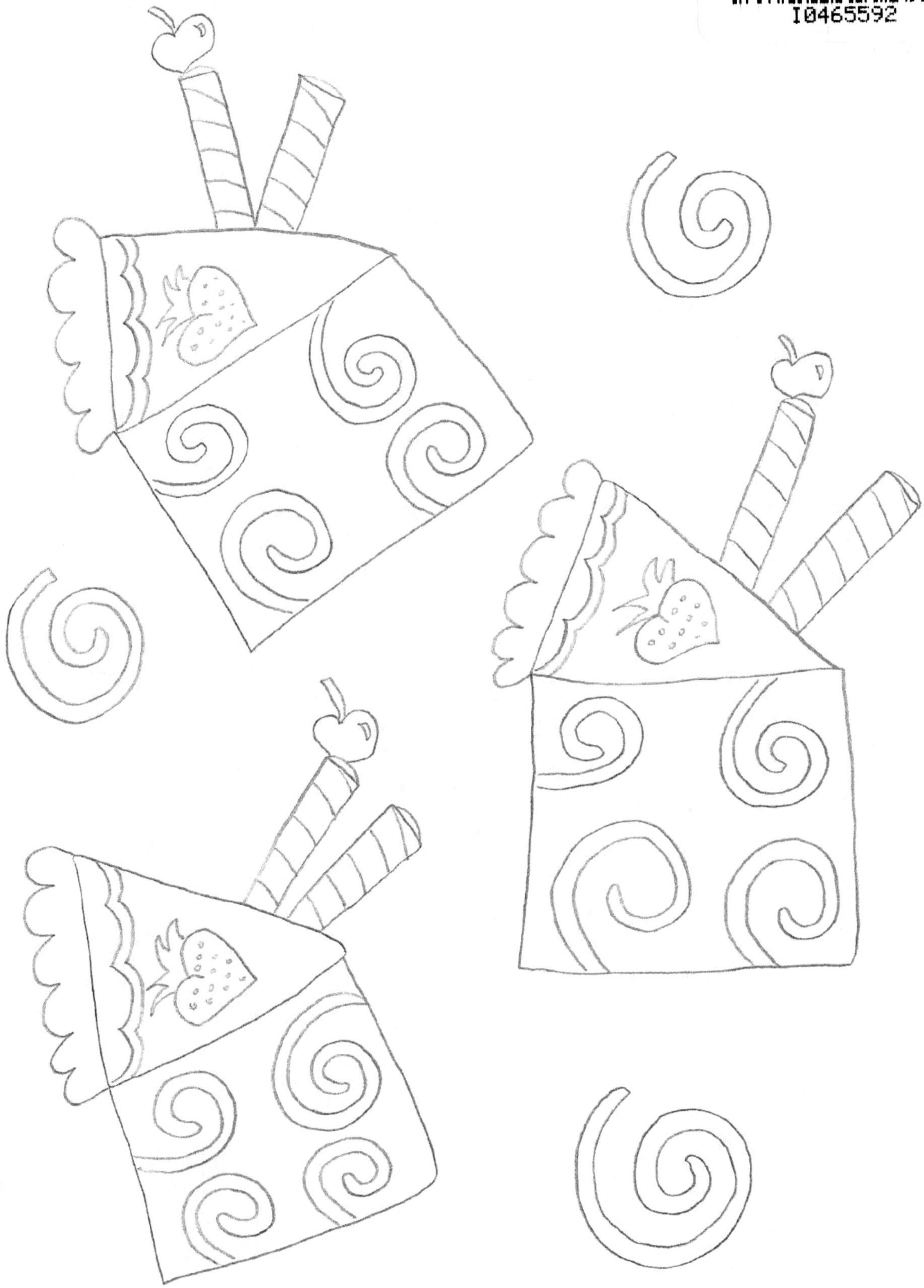

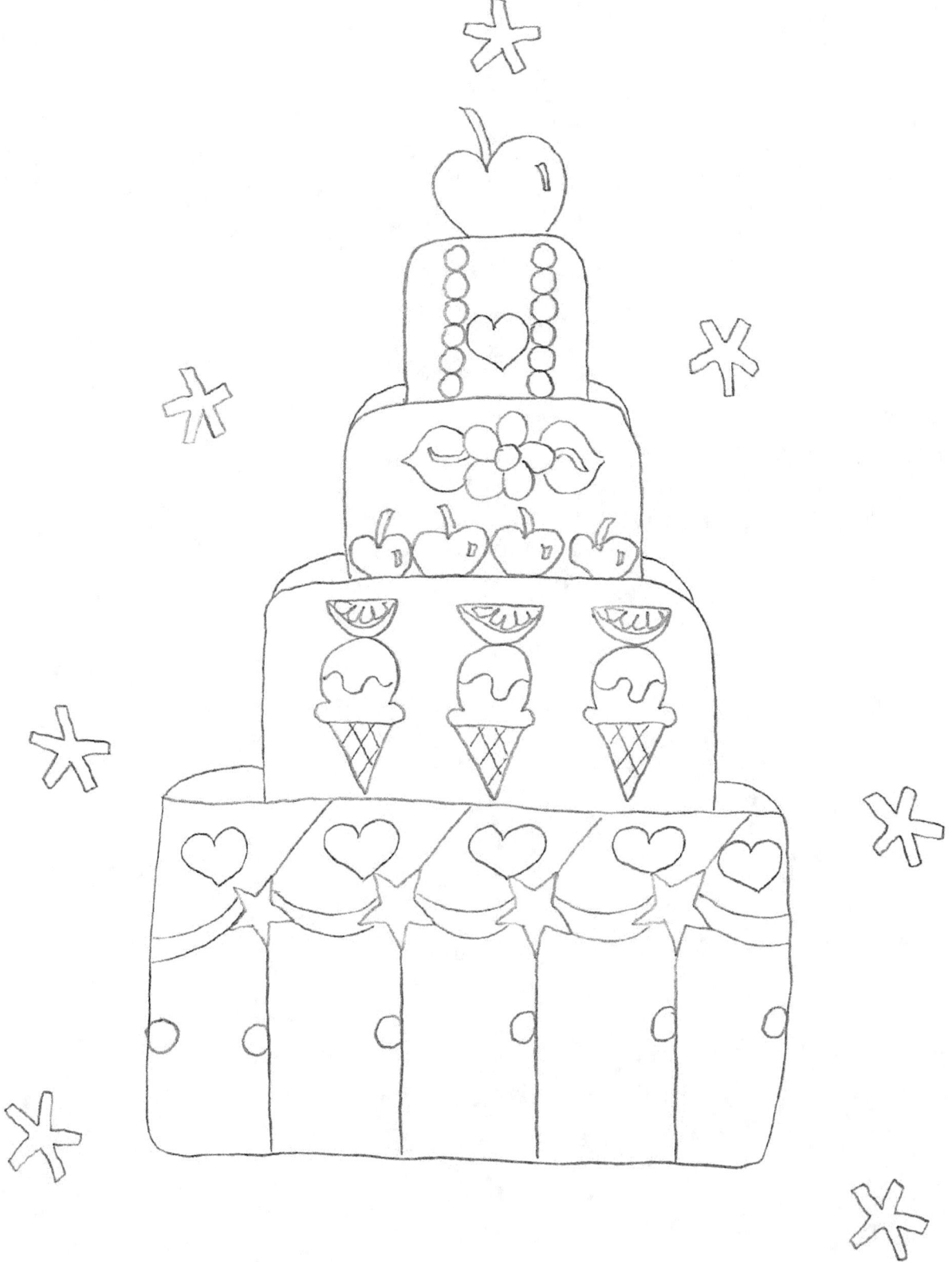

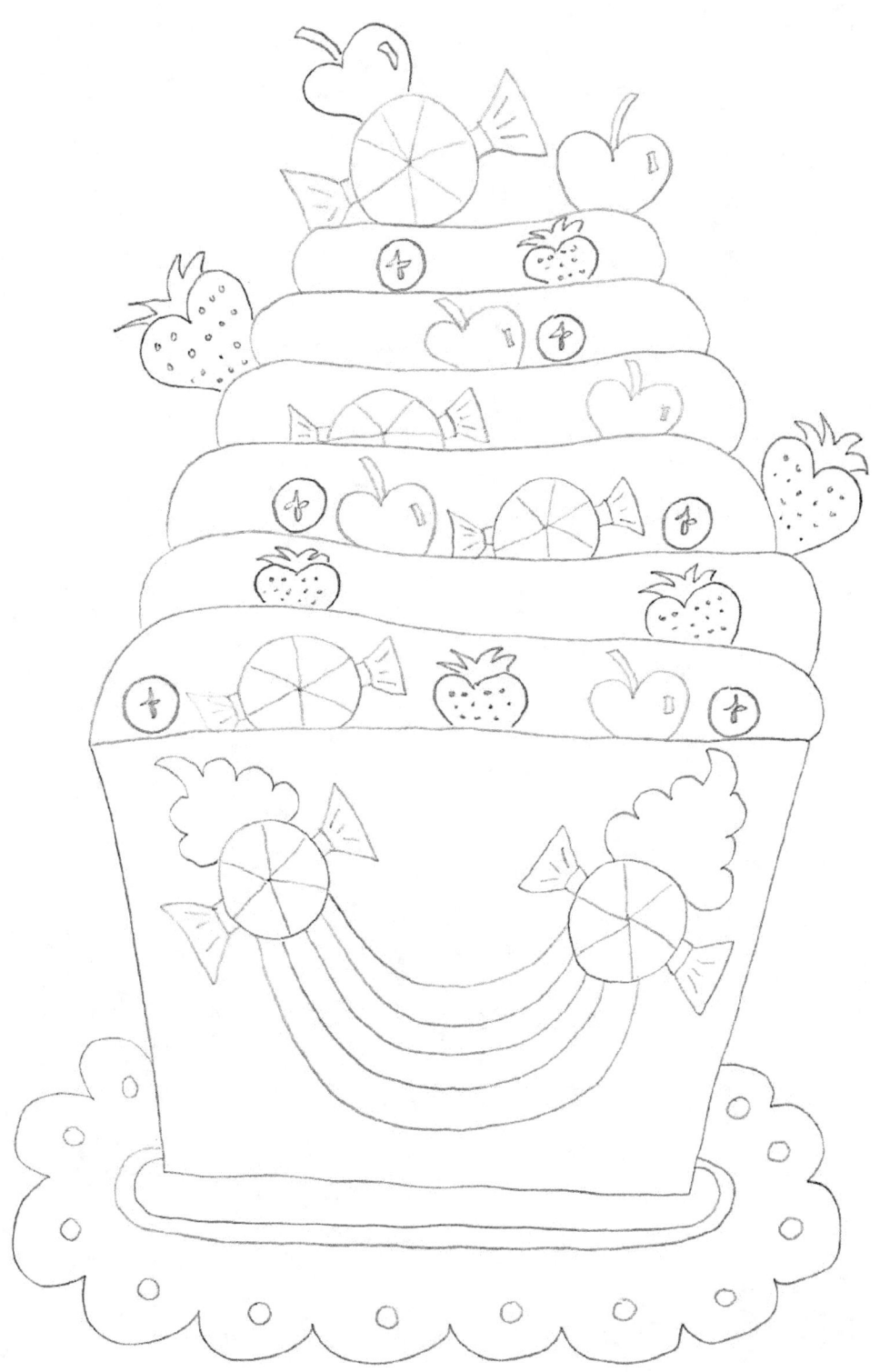

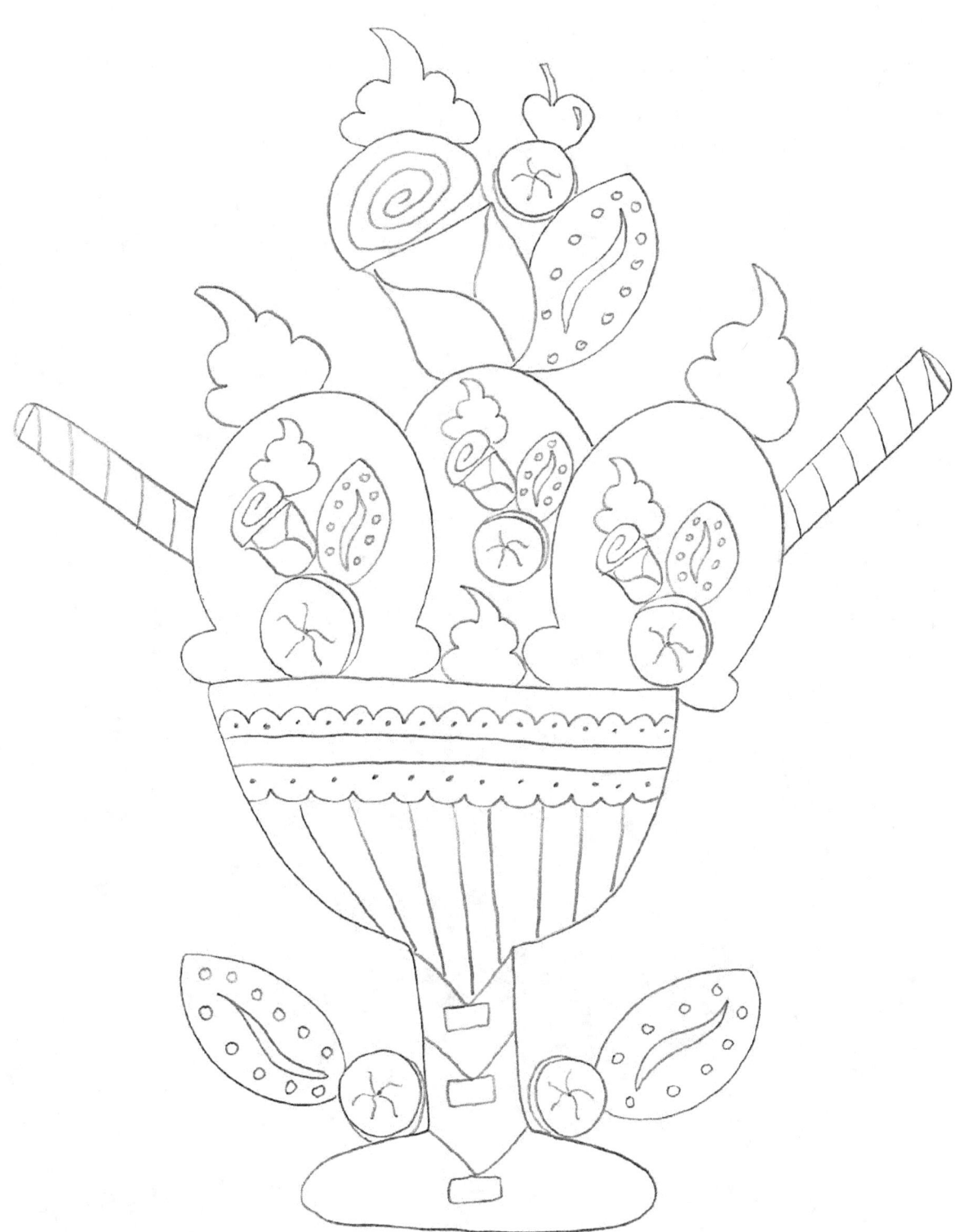

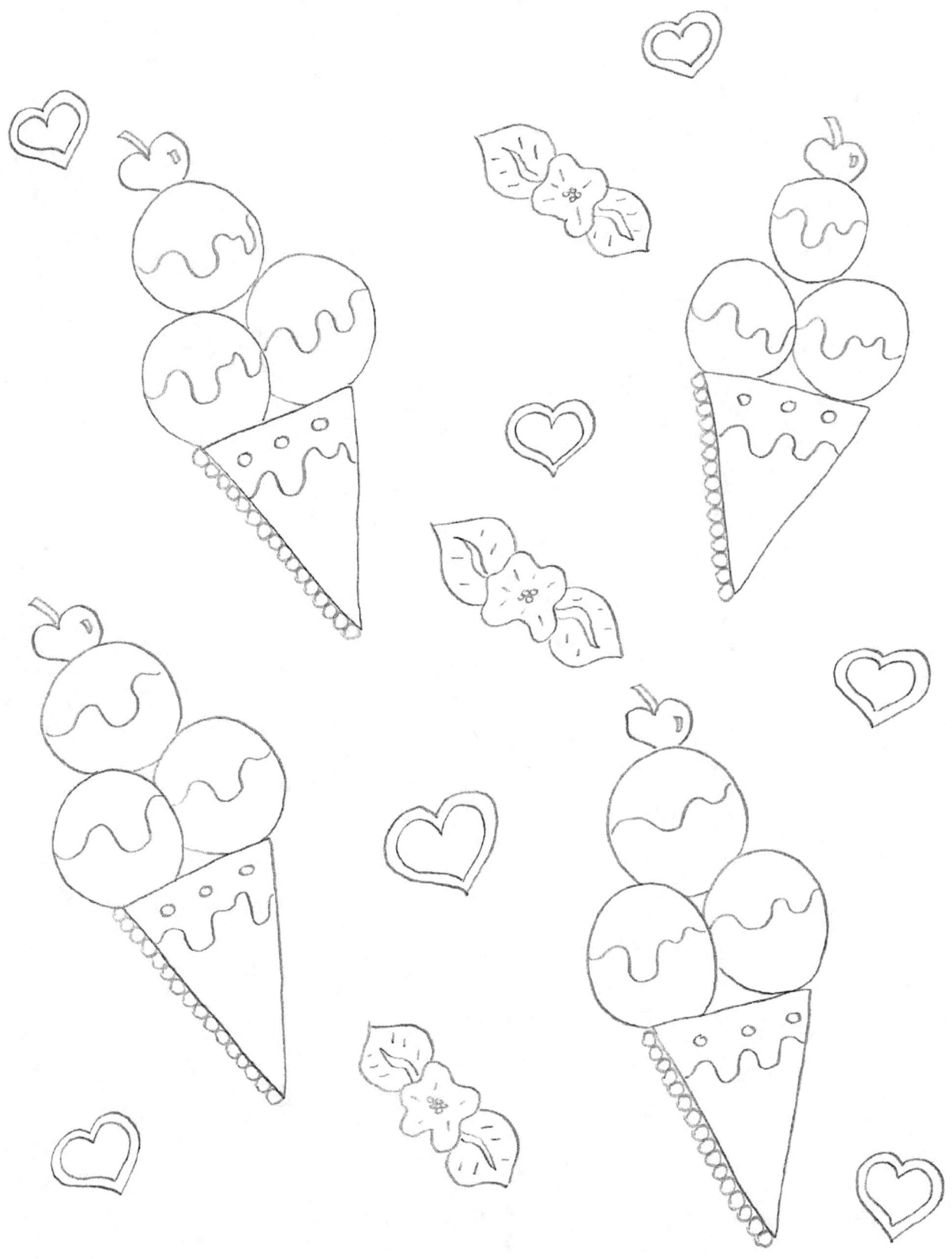

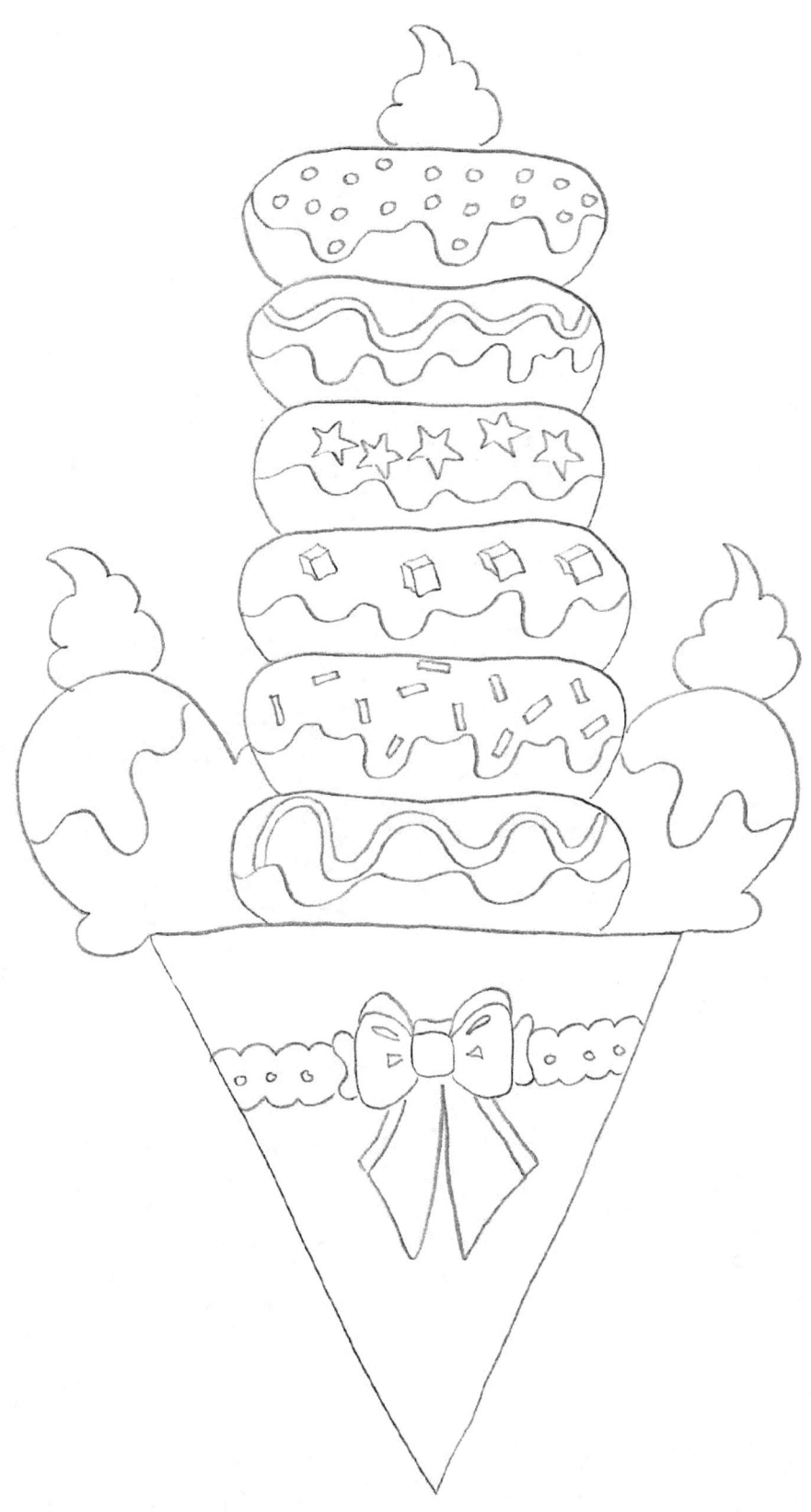

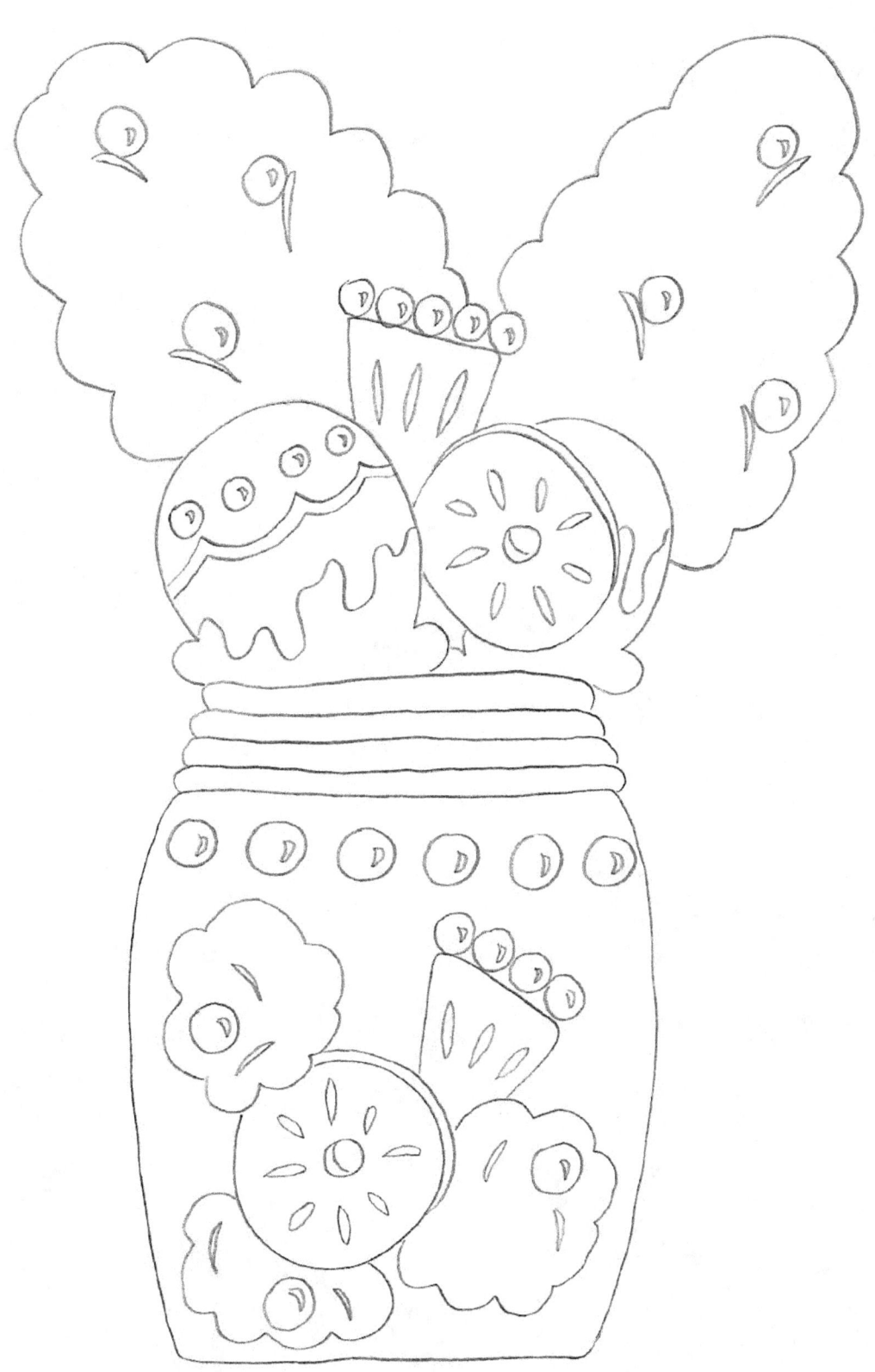

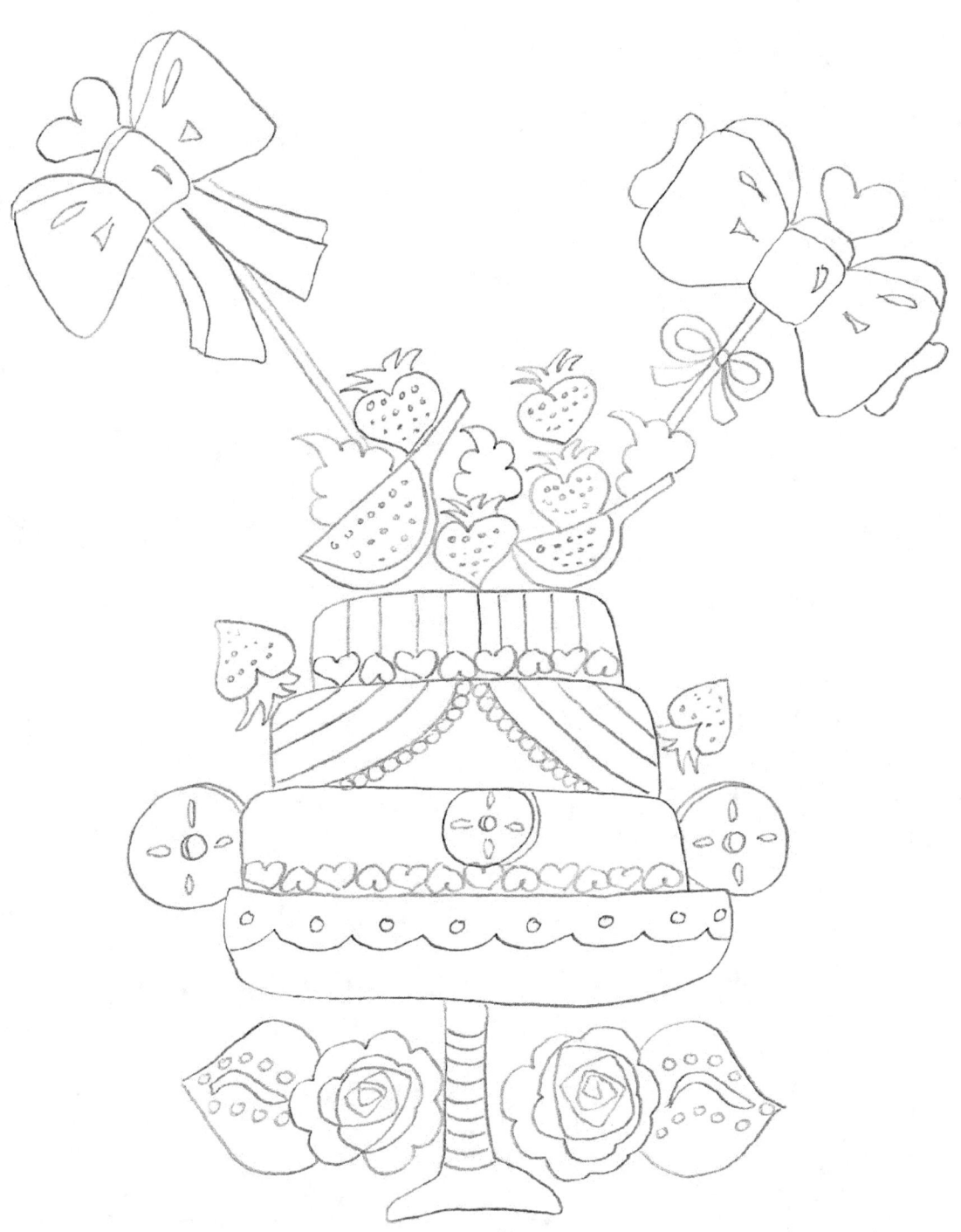

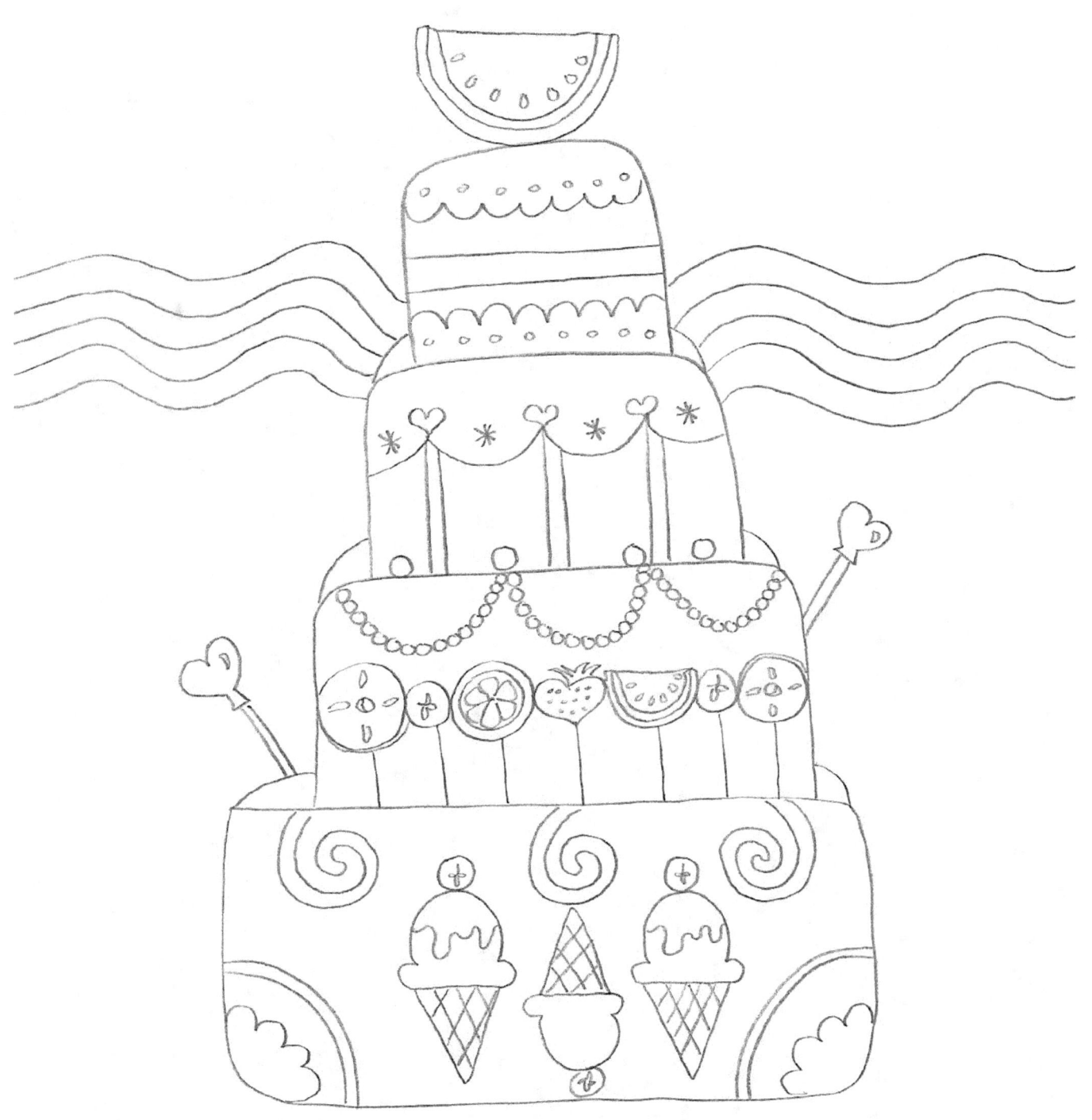

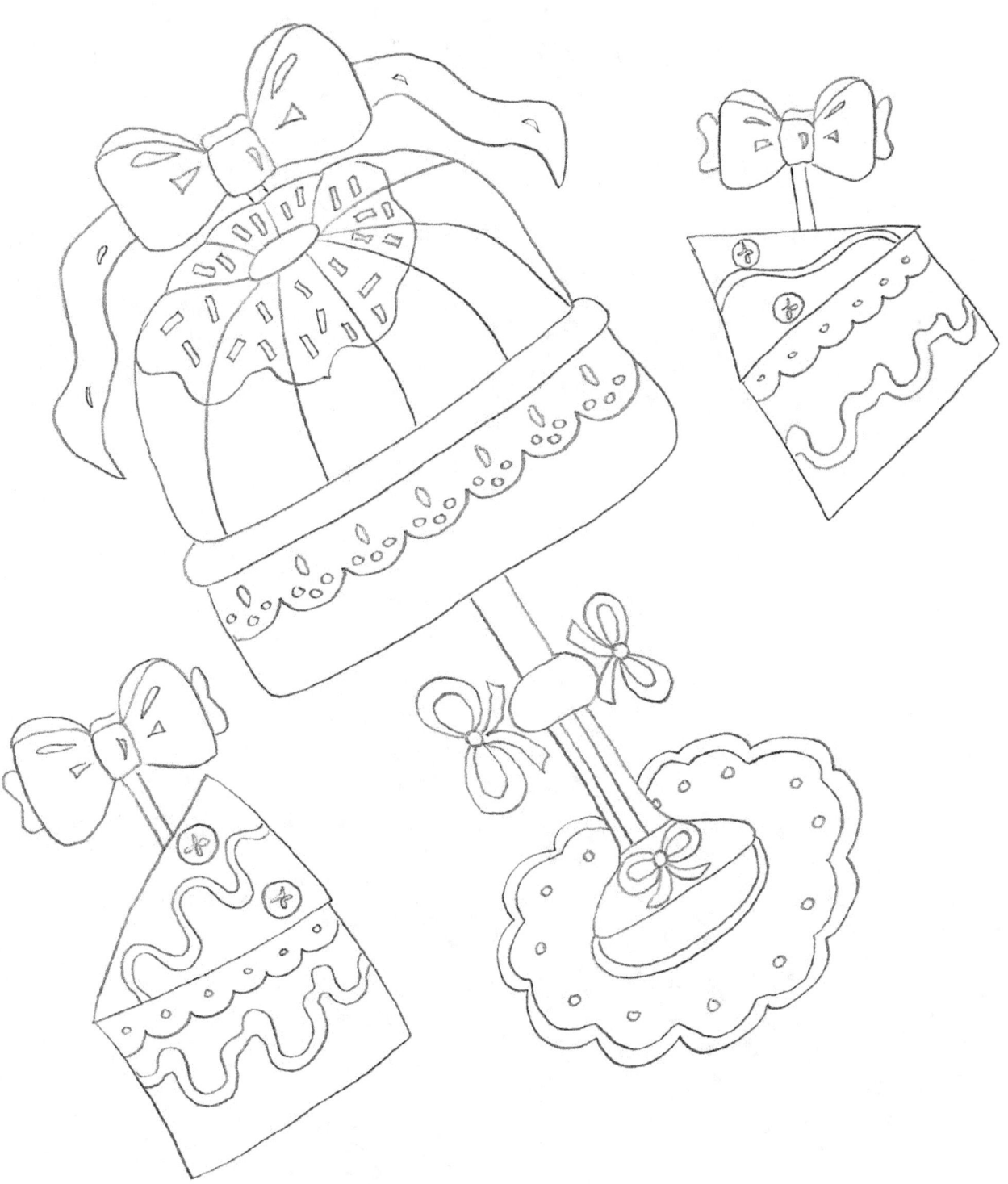

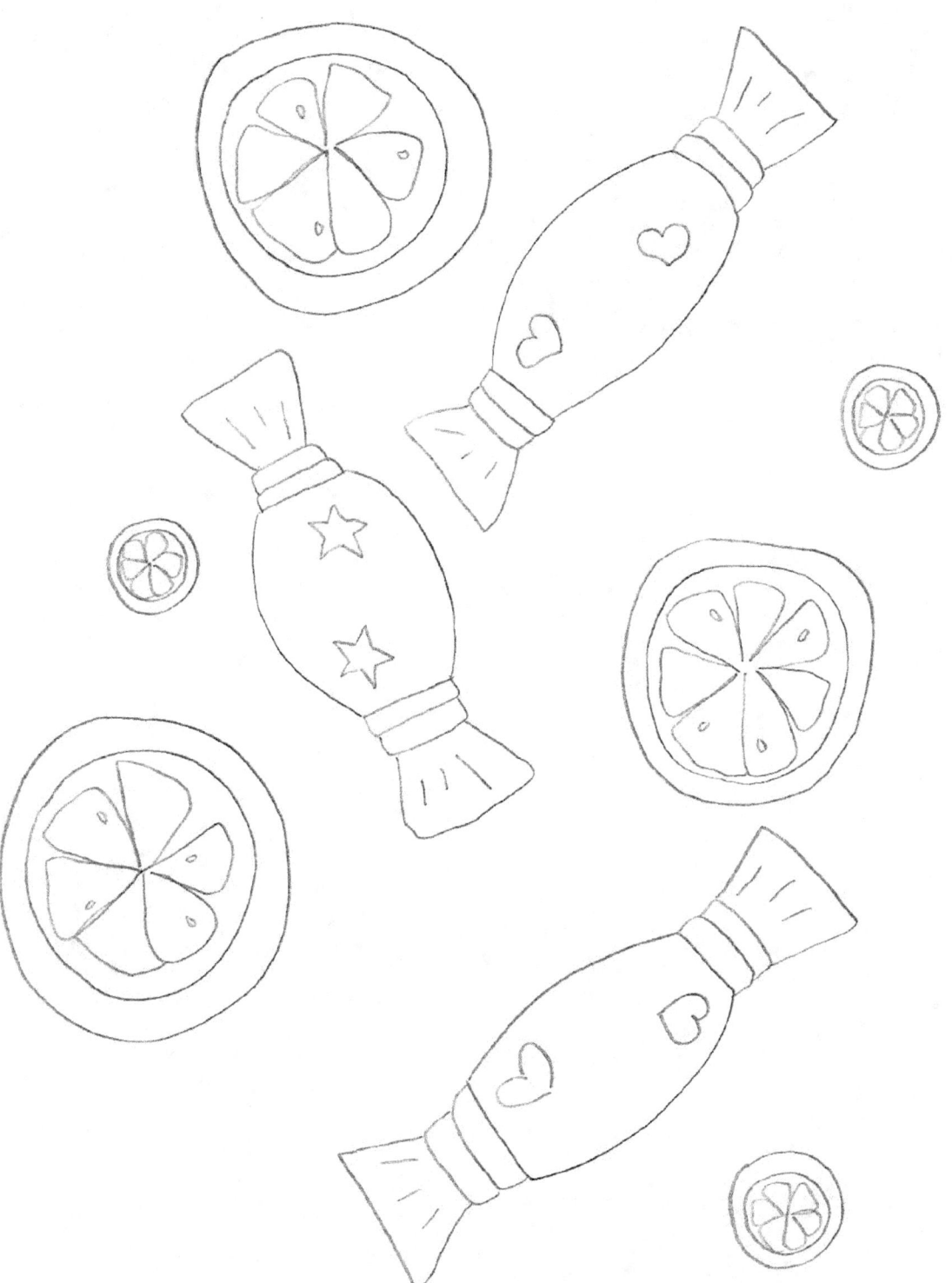

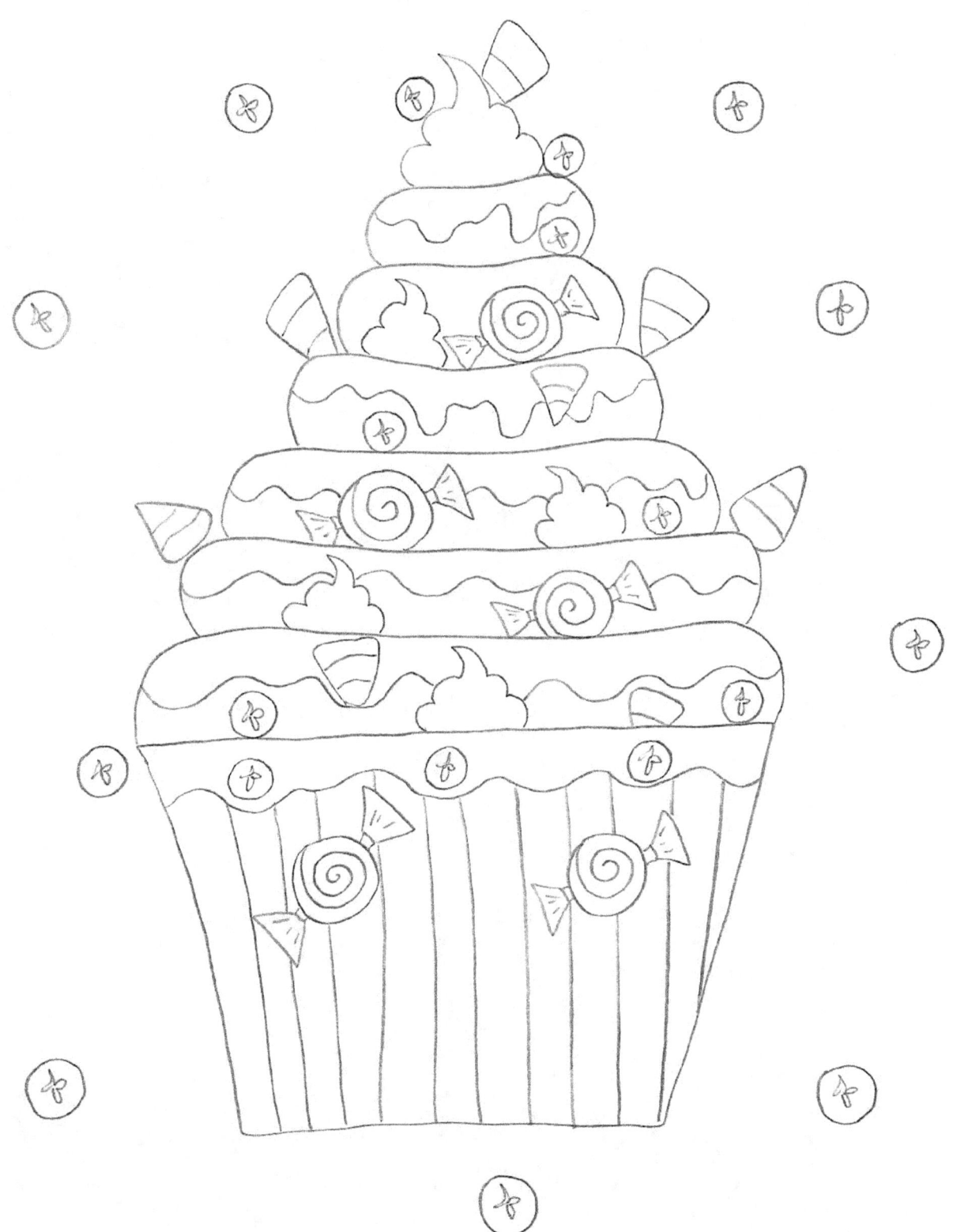

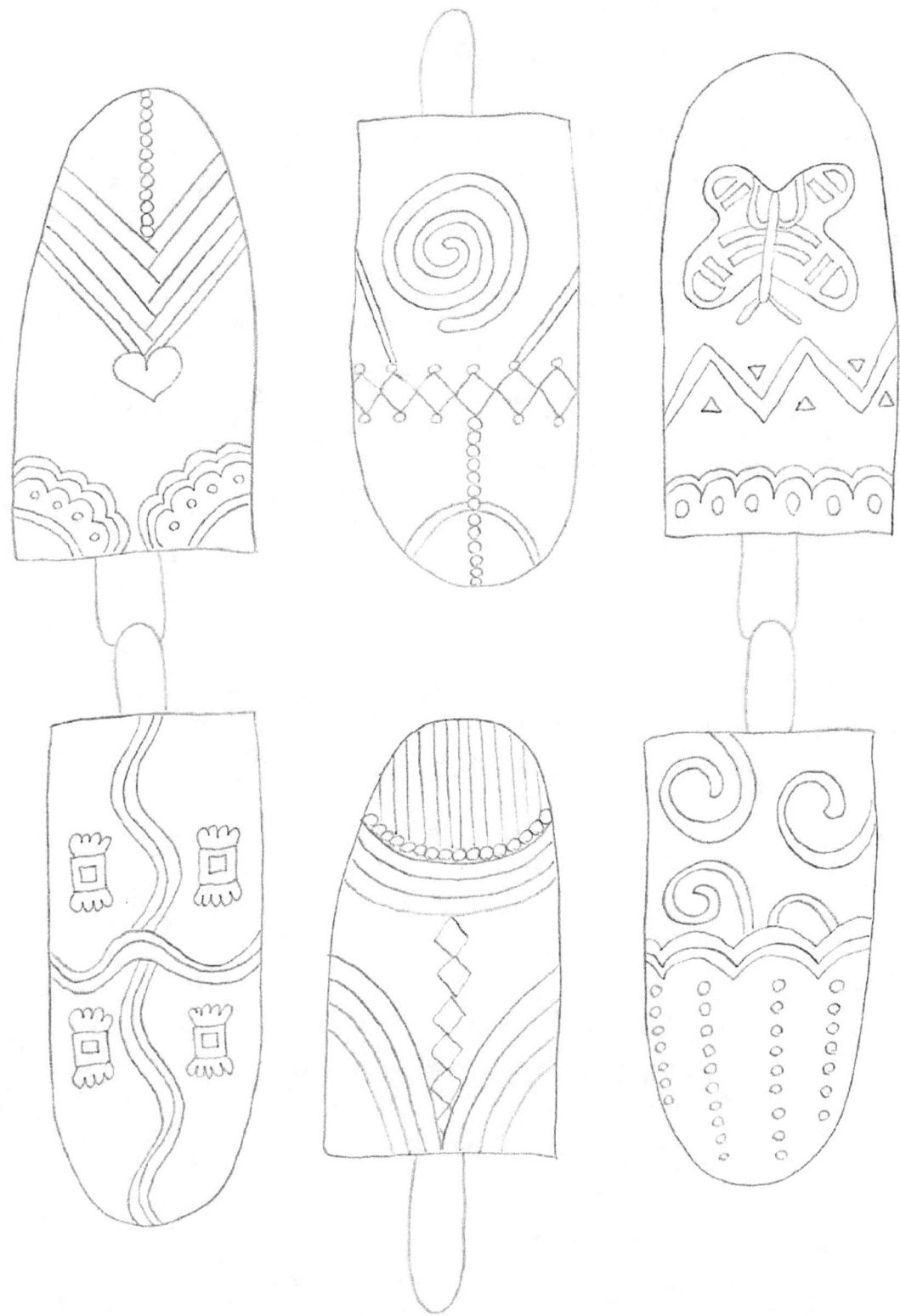

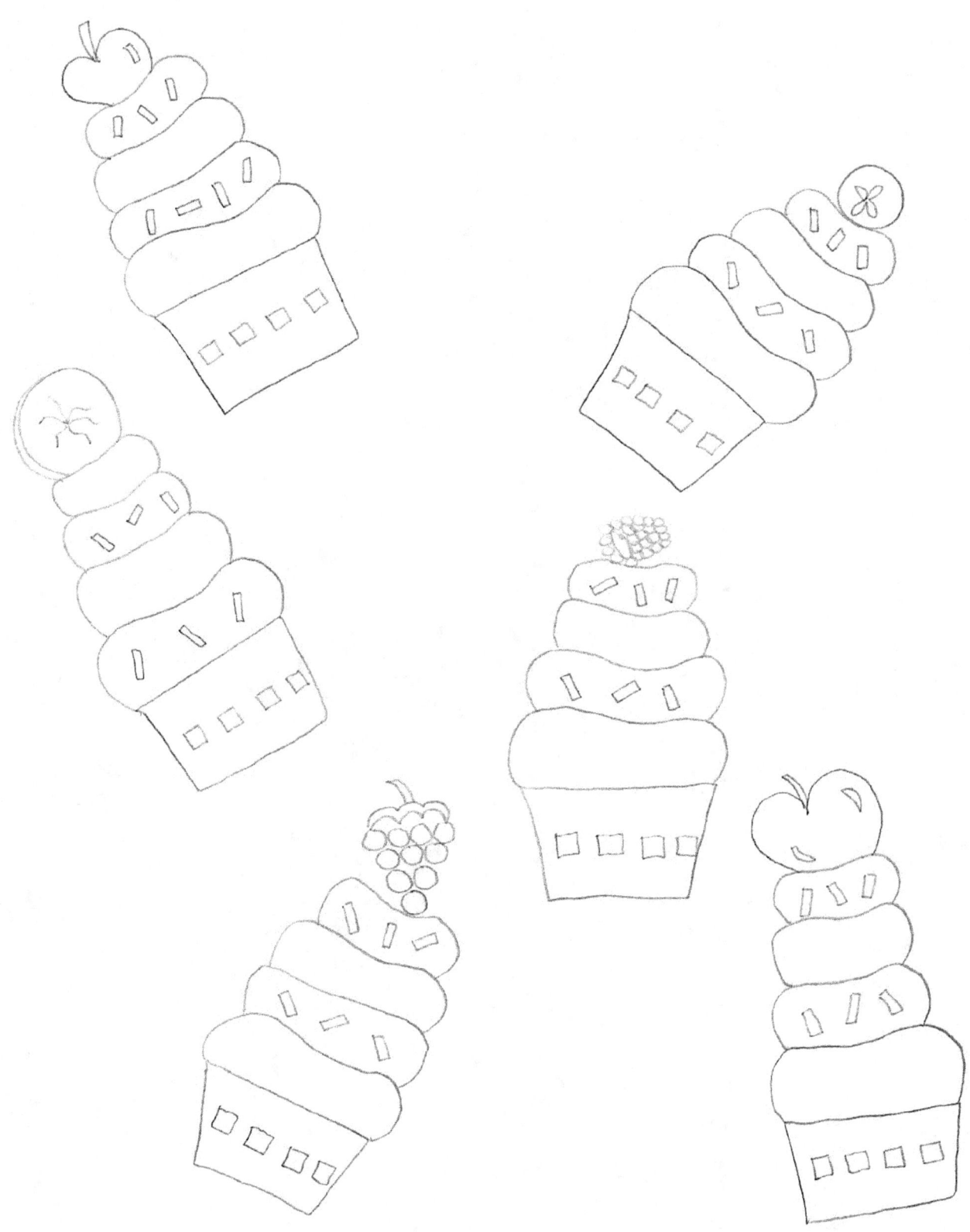

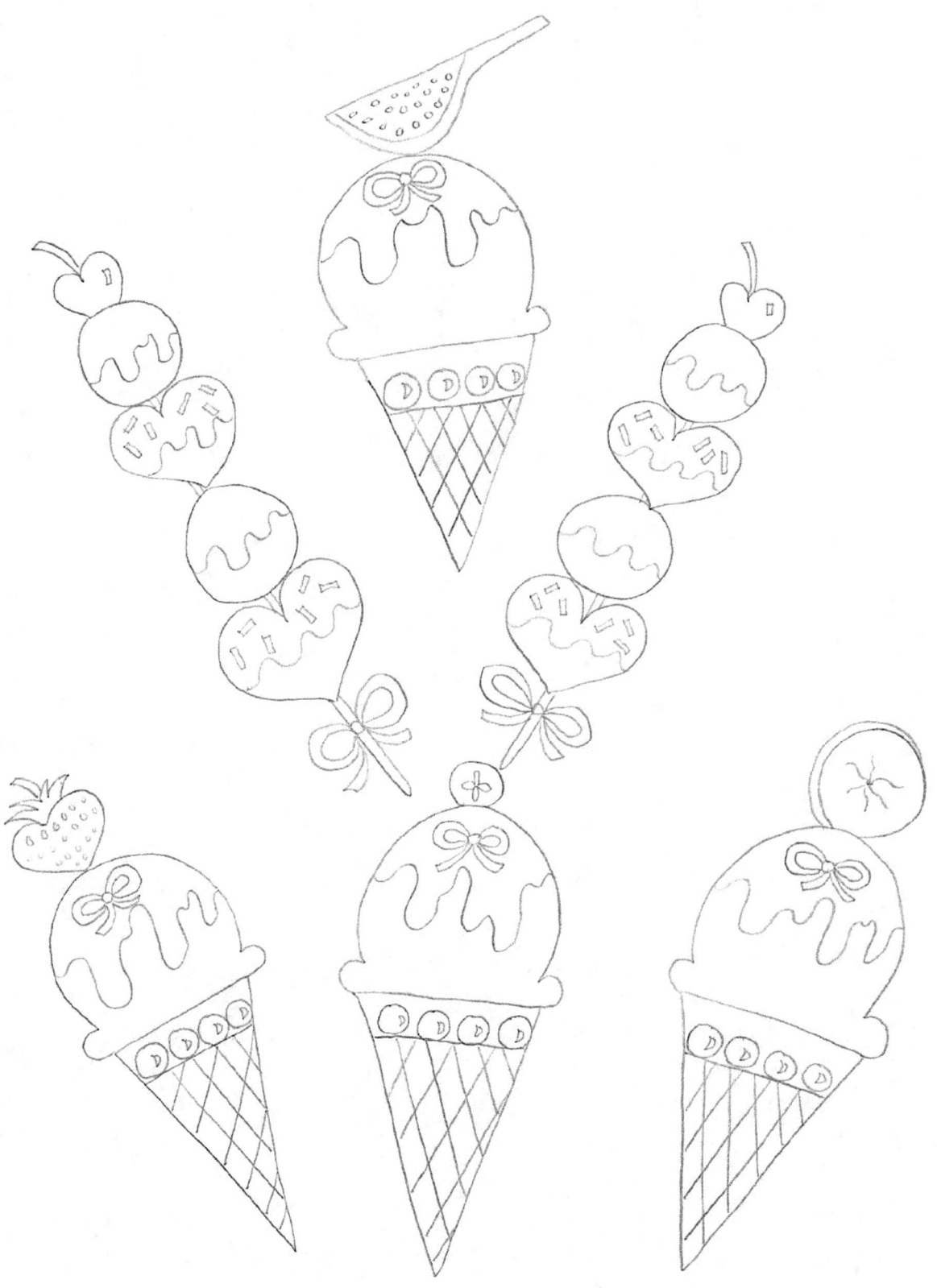

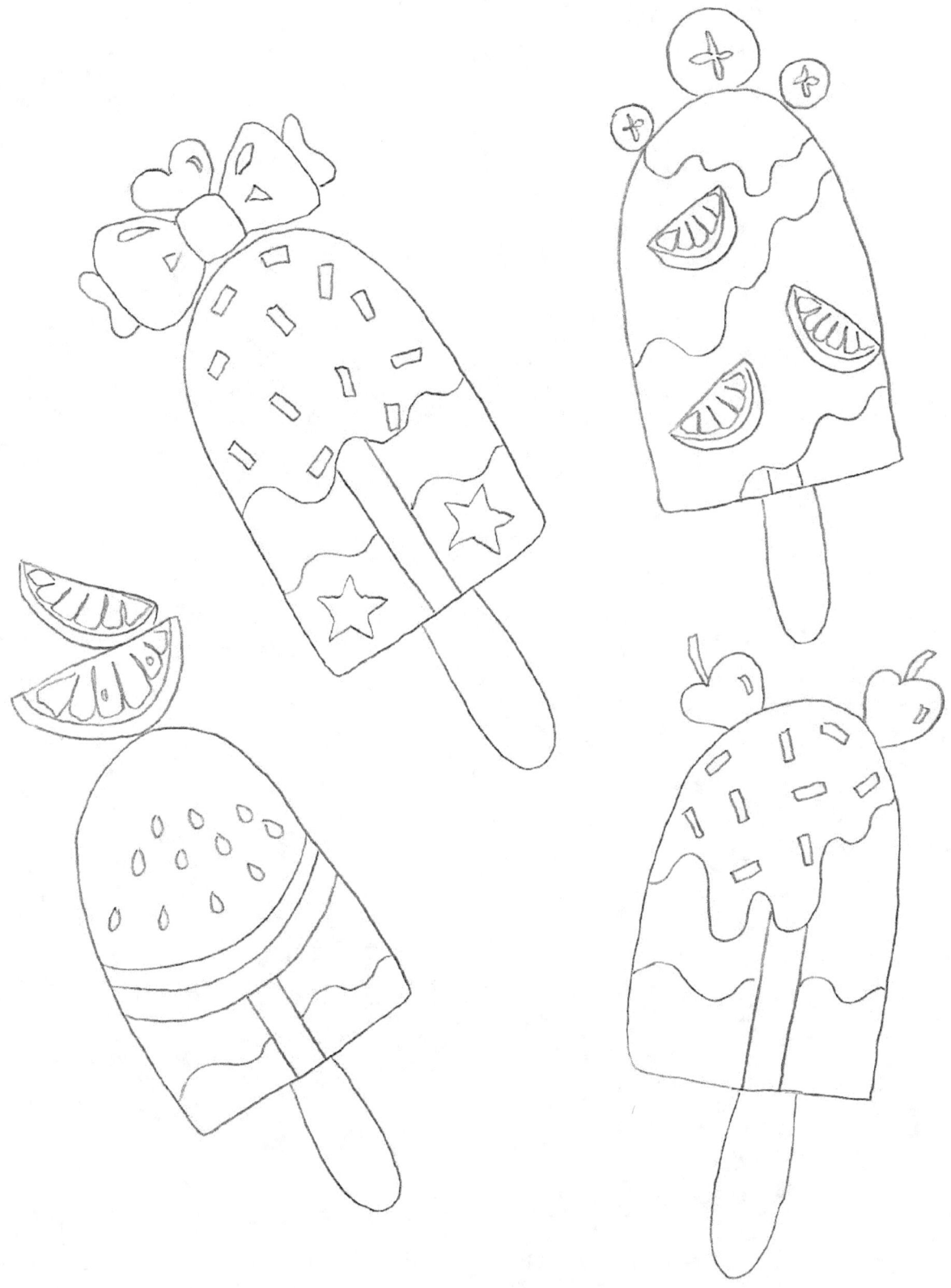

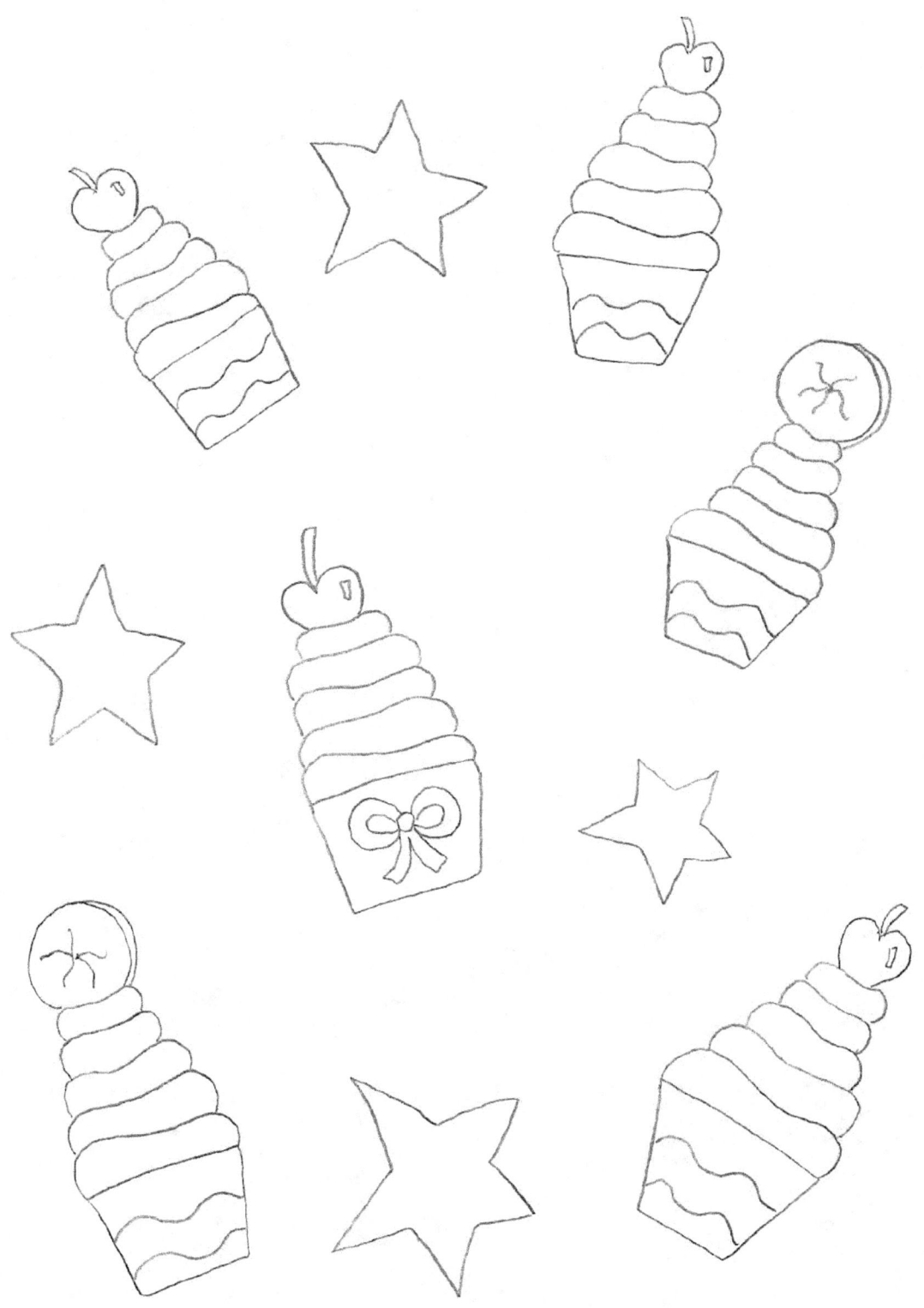

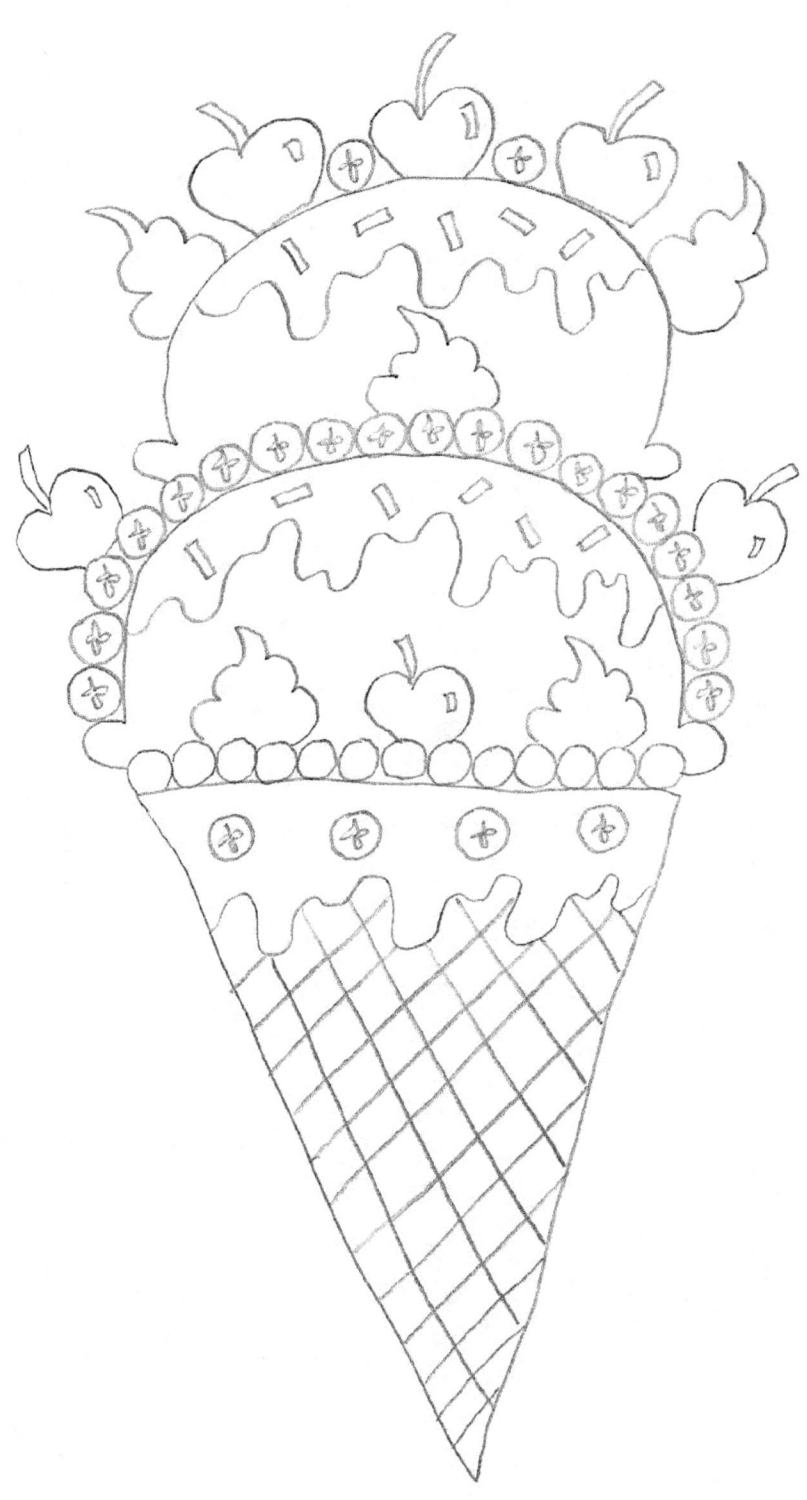

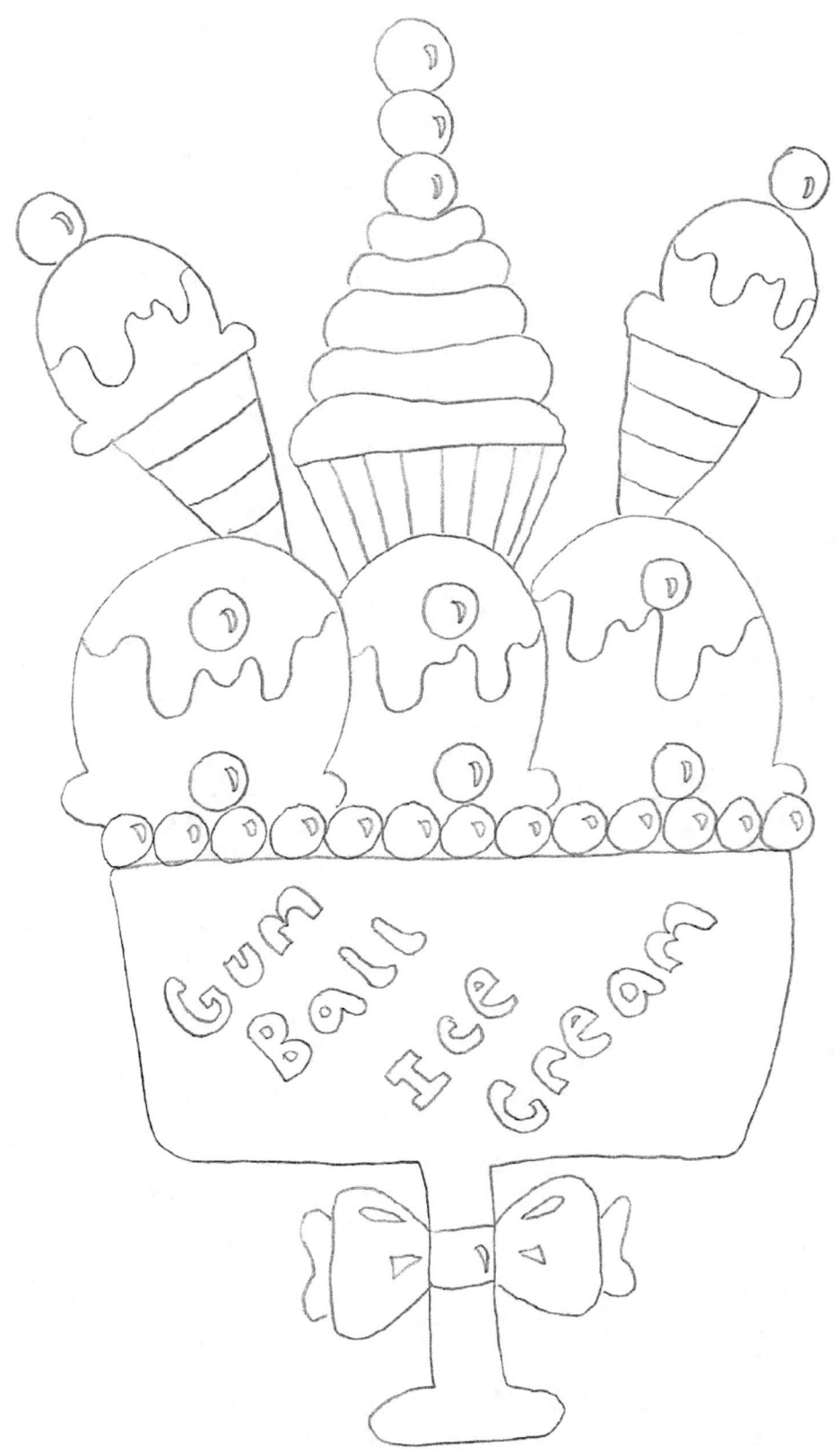

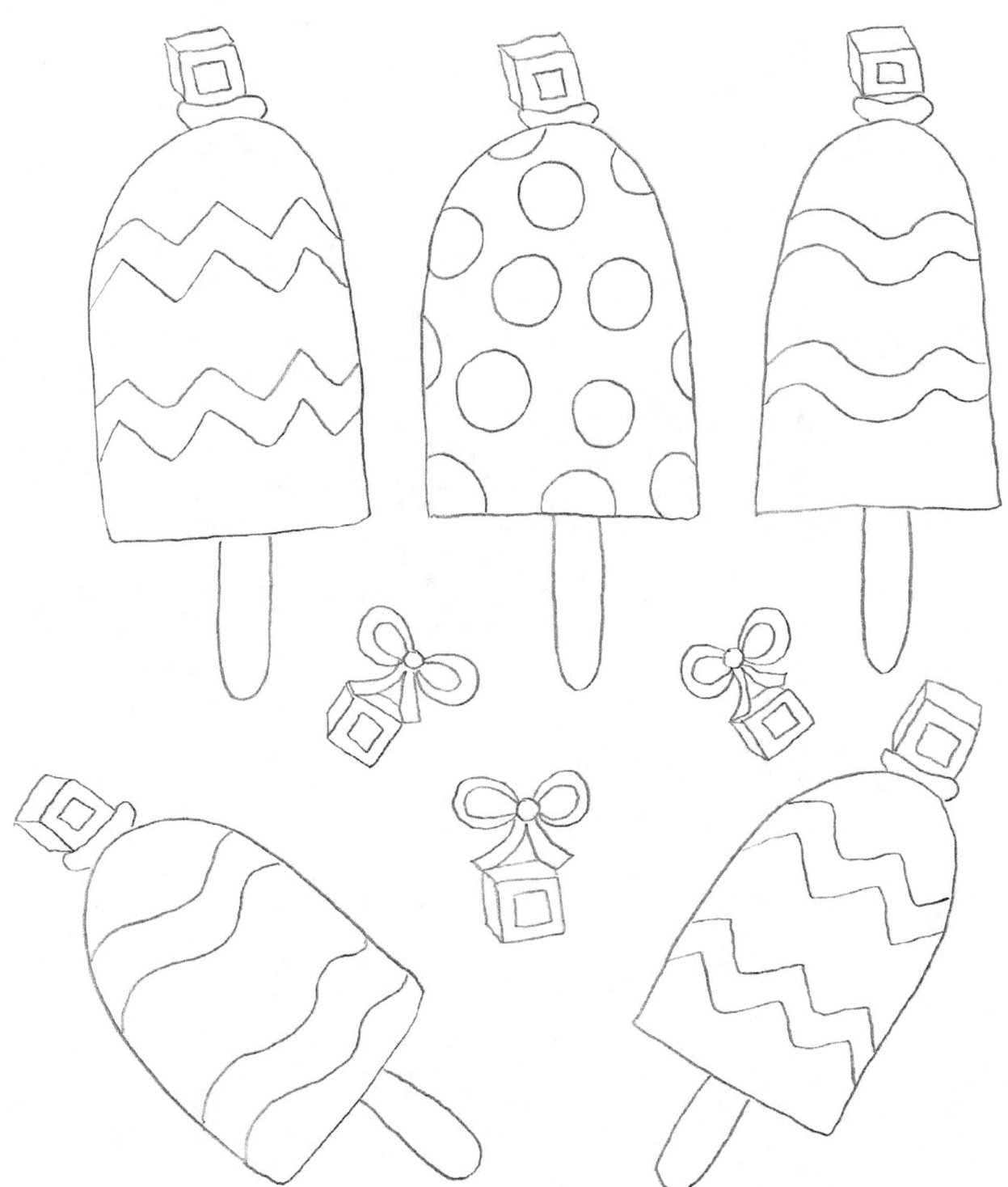

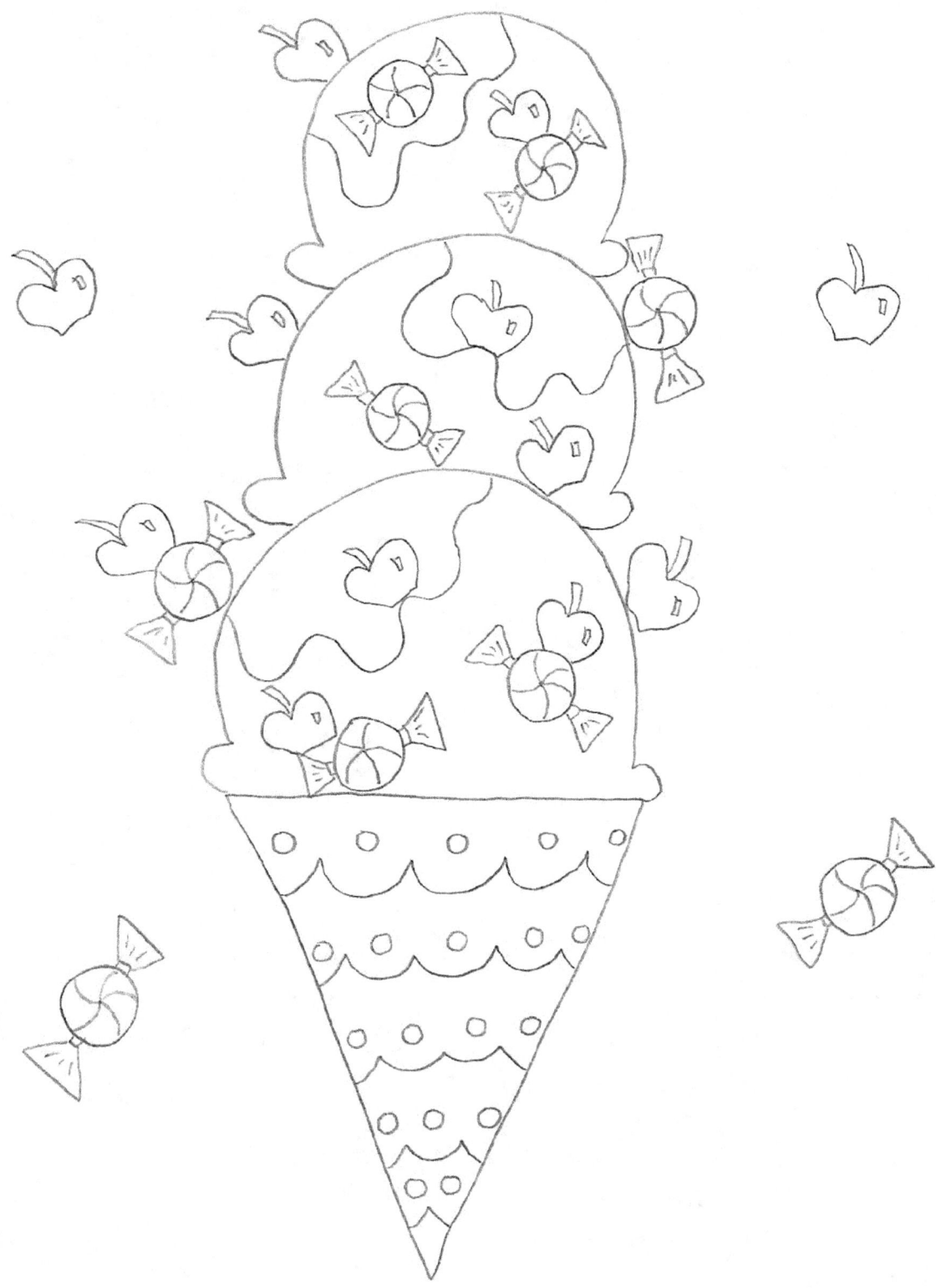

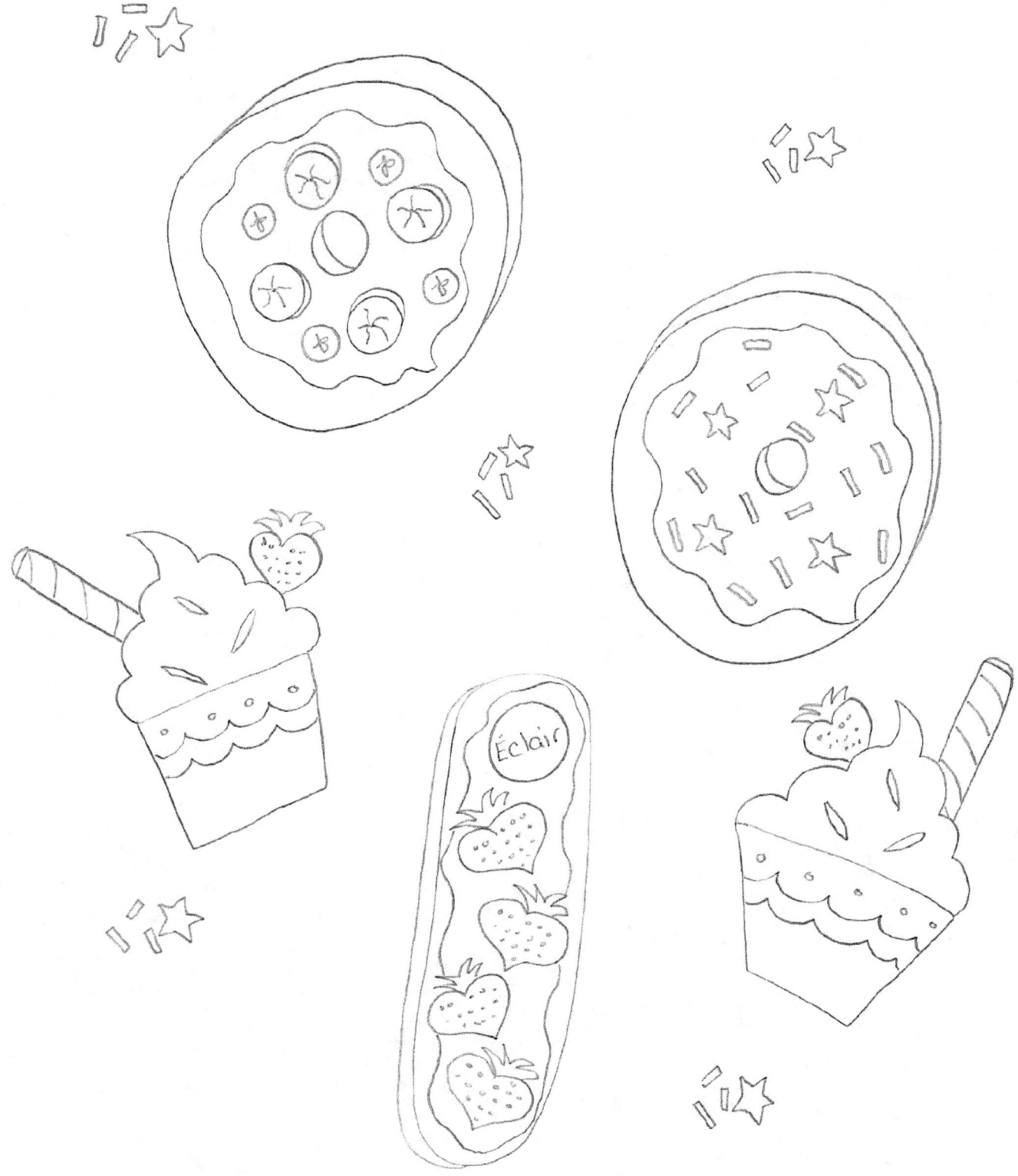

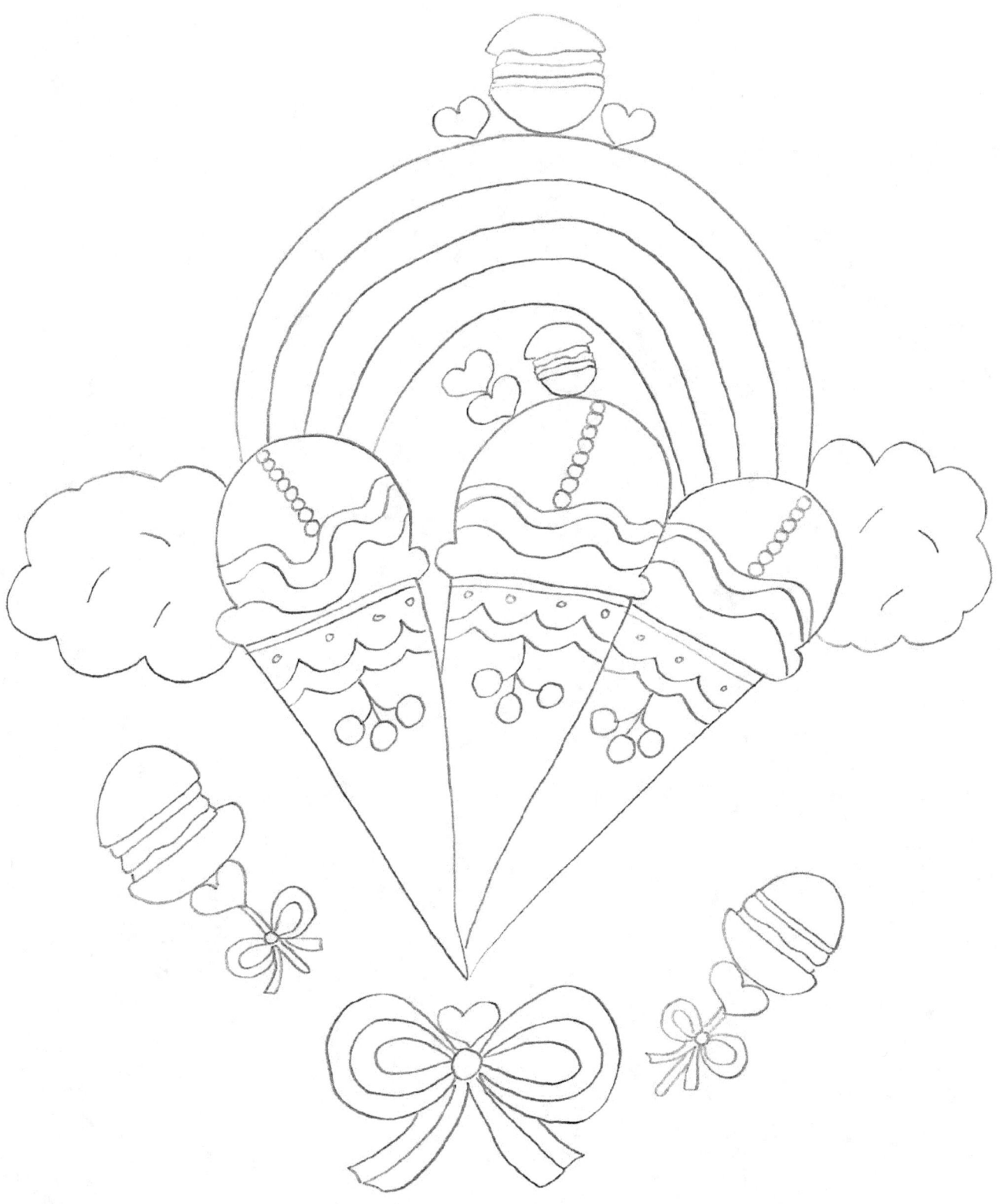

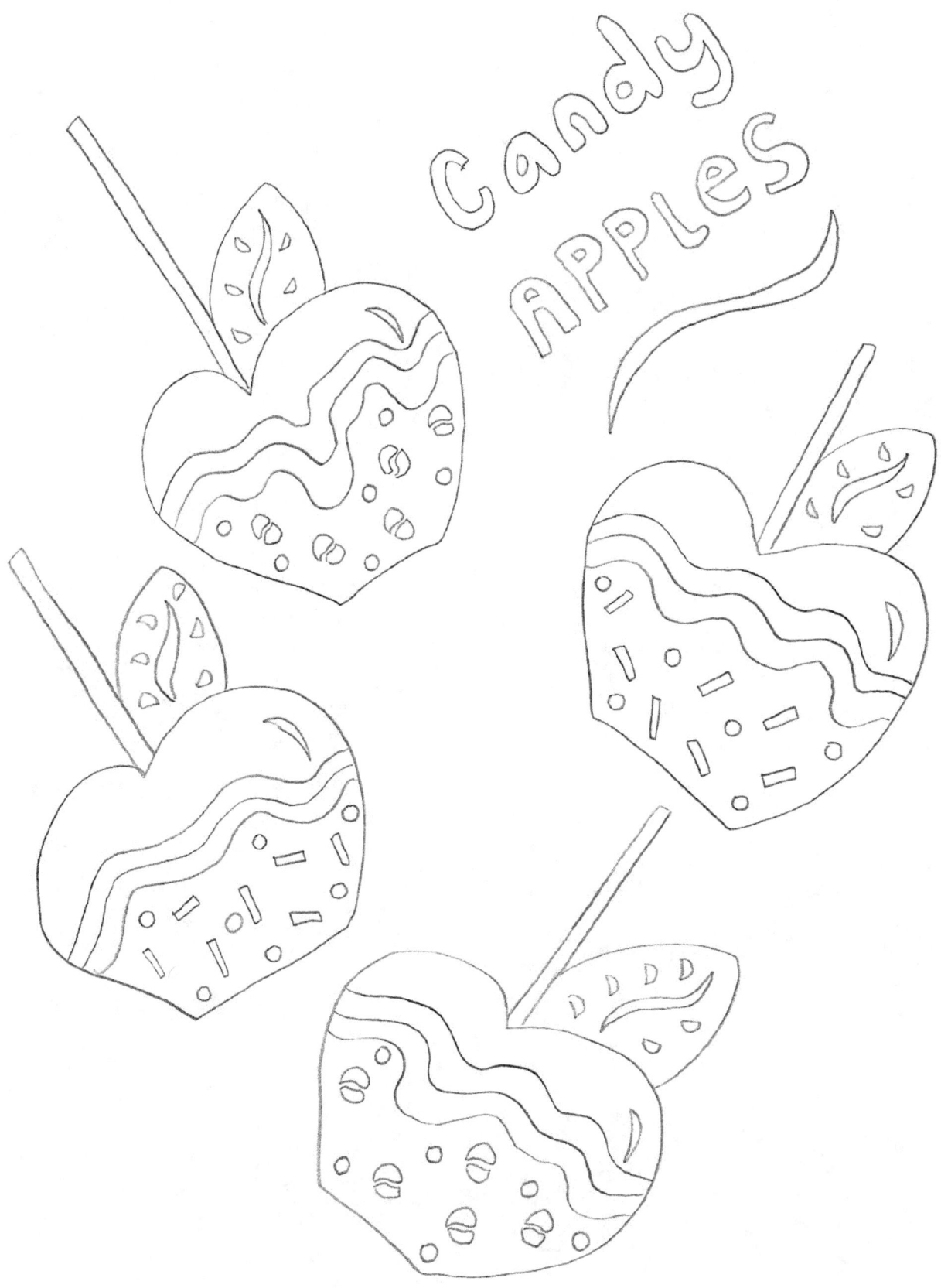

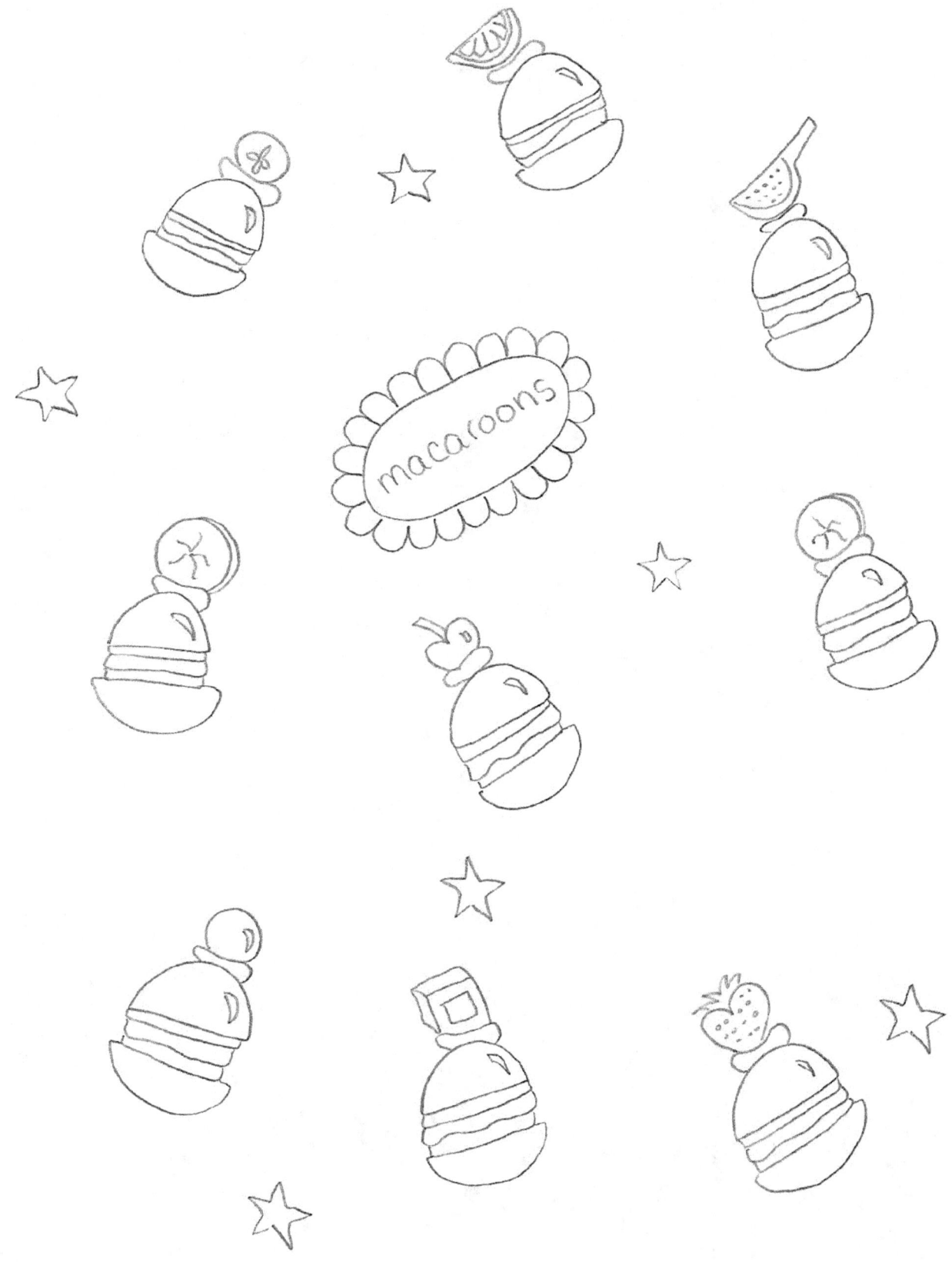

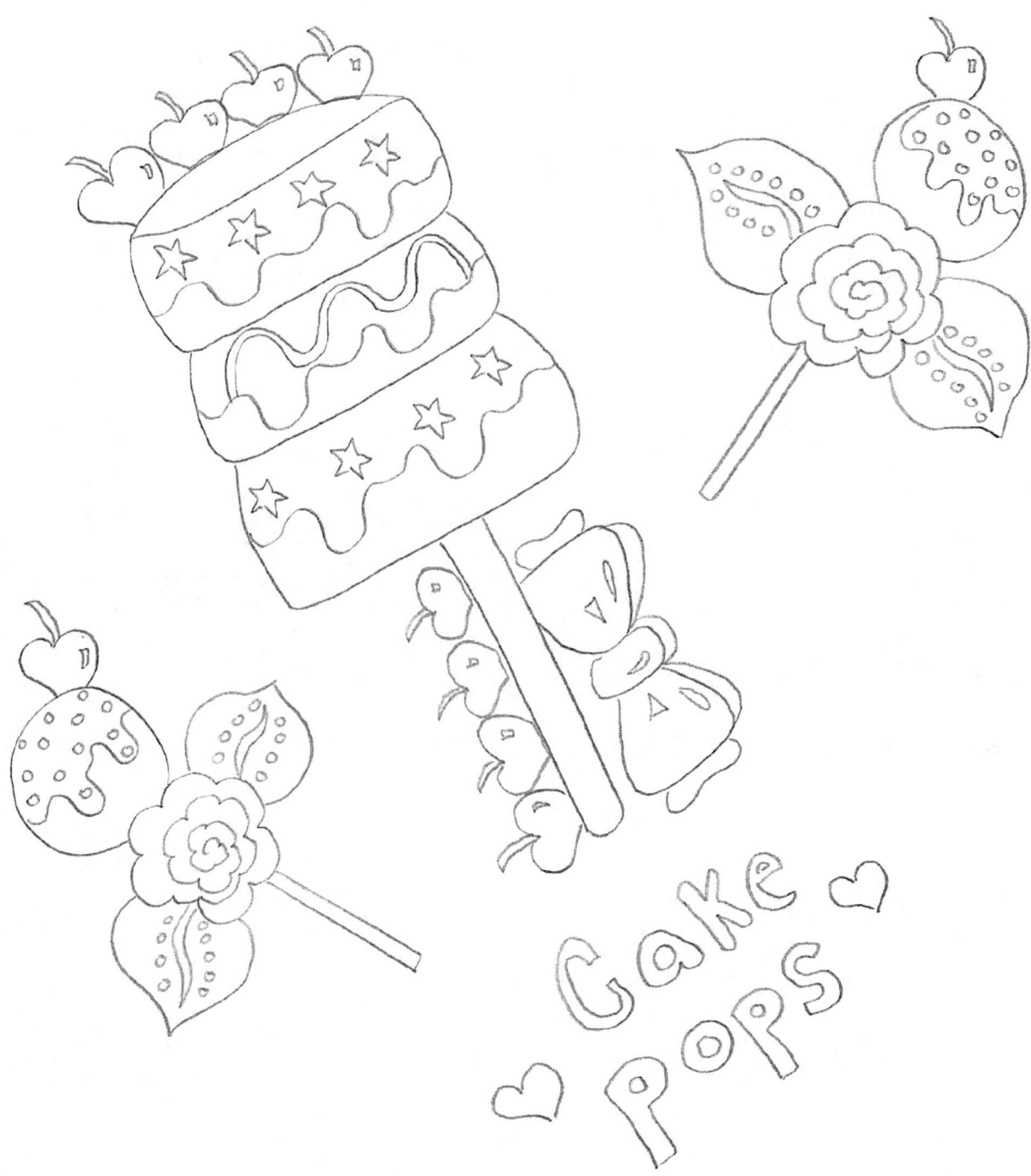

Cake ♥
Pops ♥

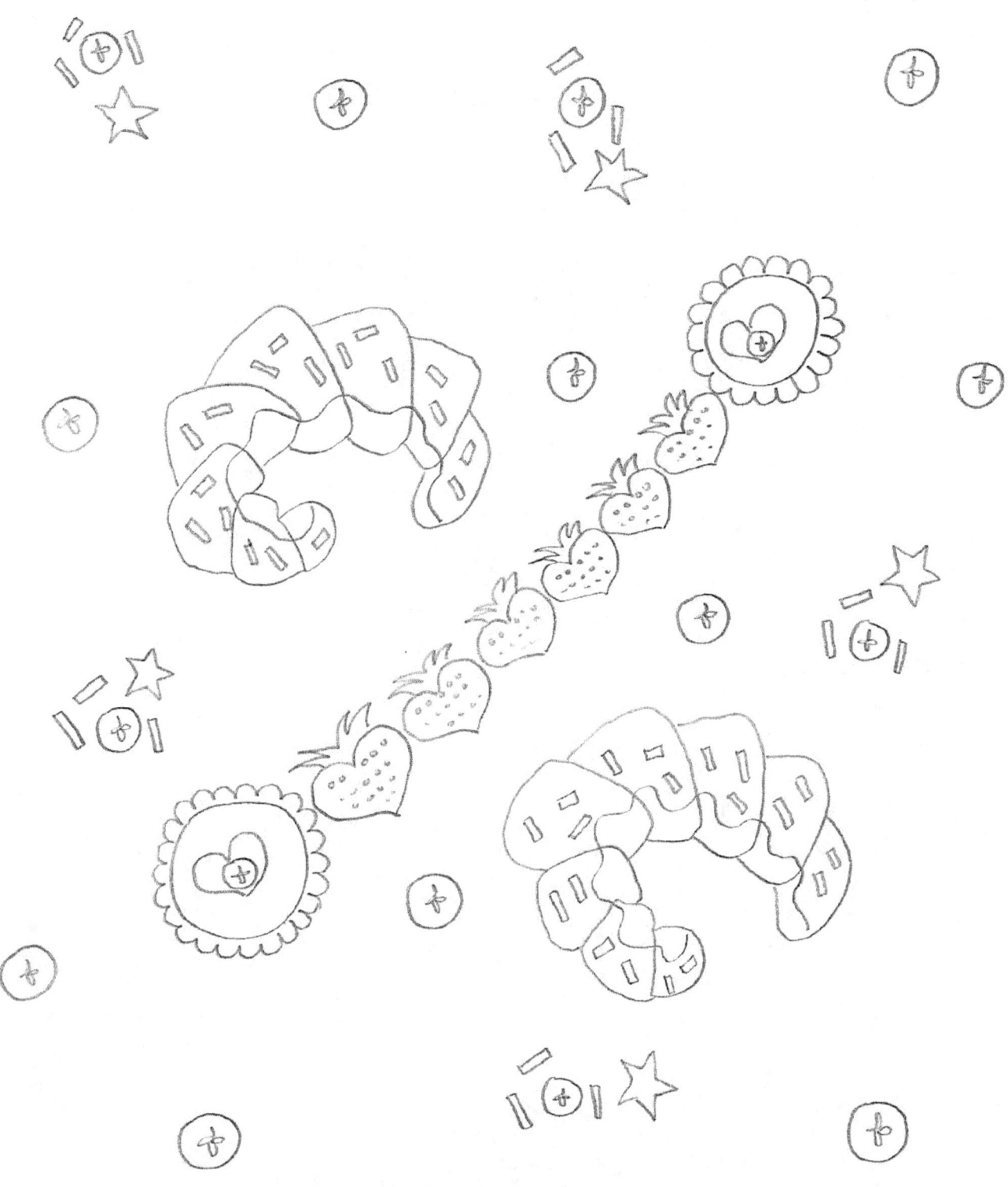

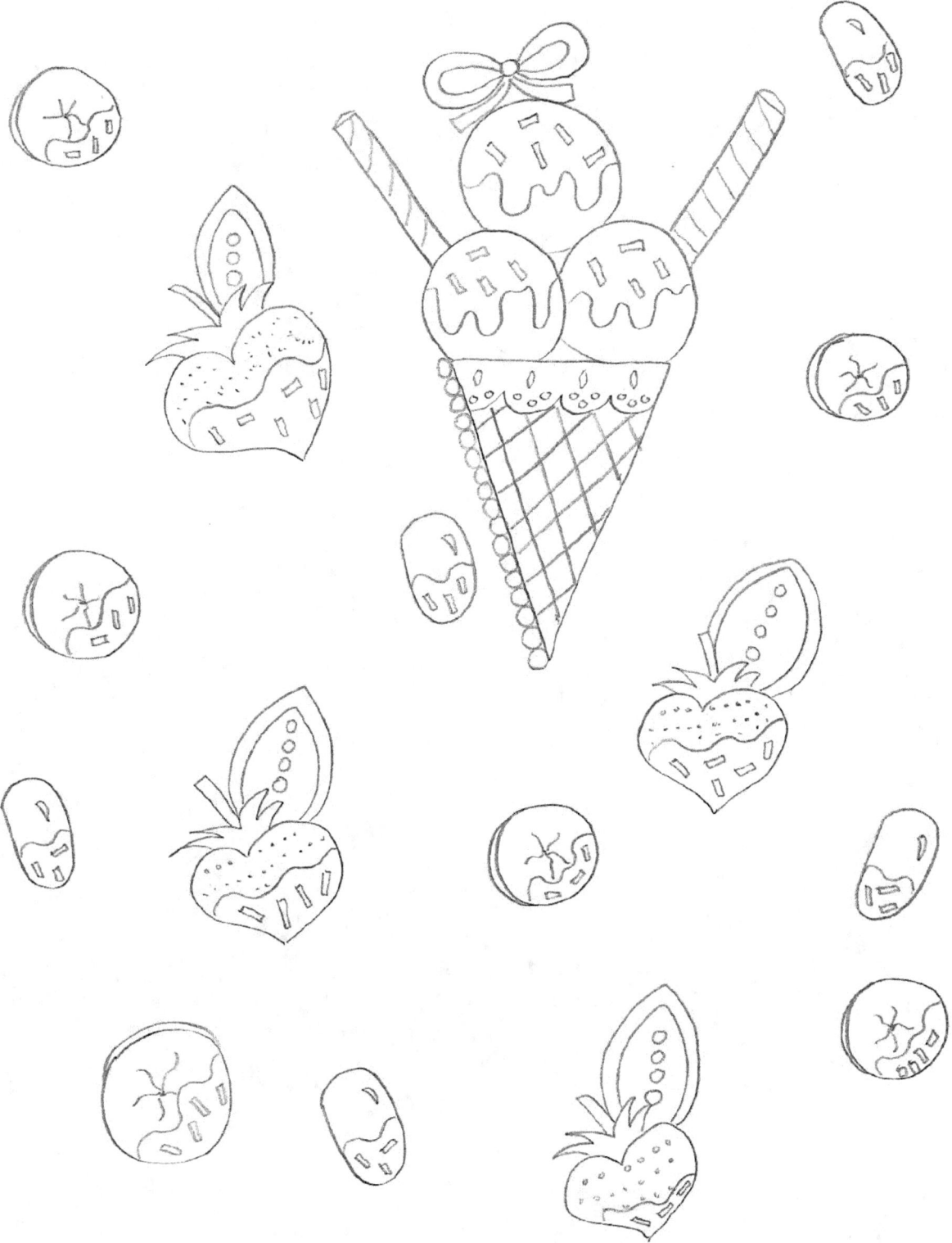

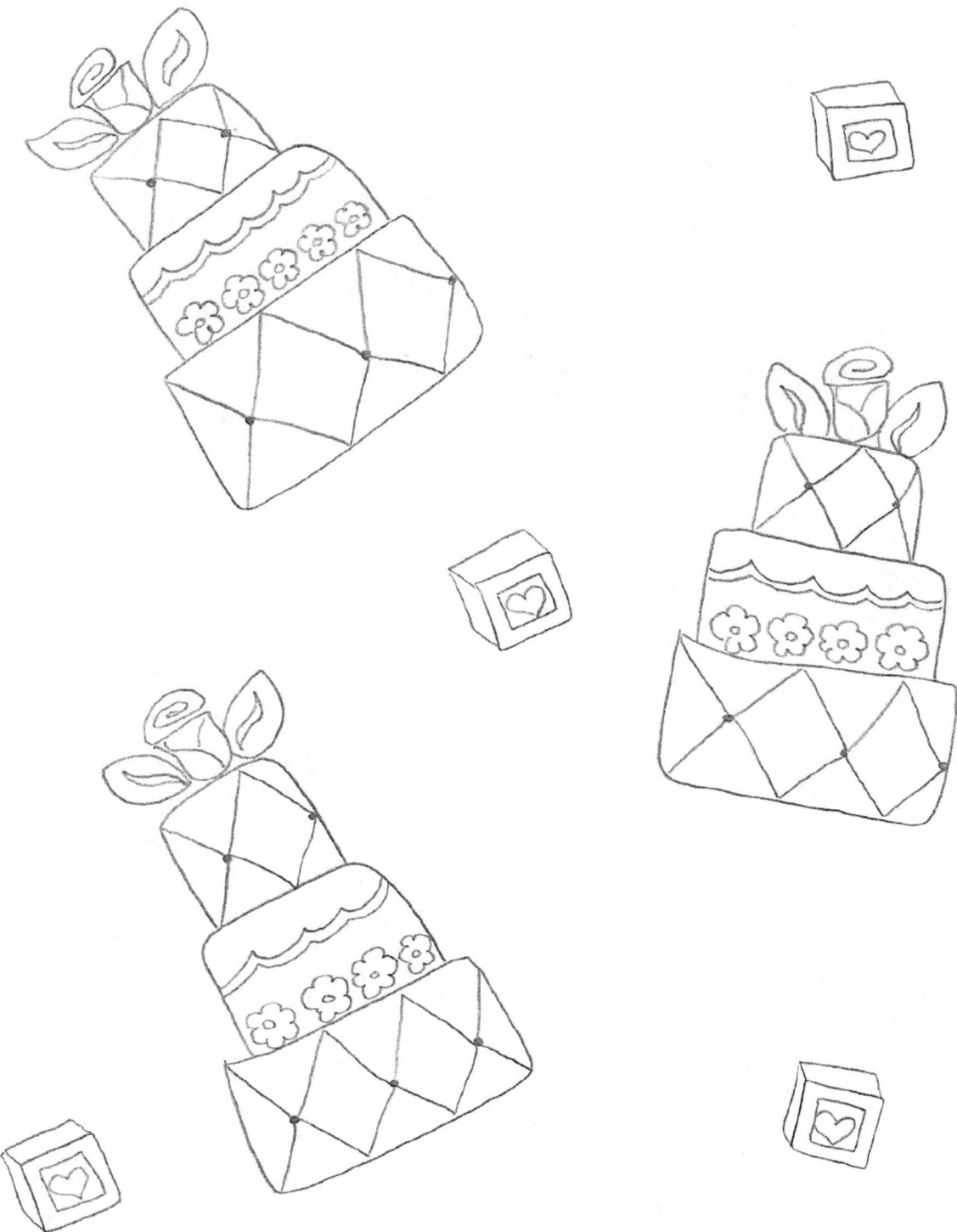

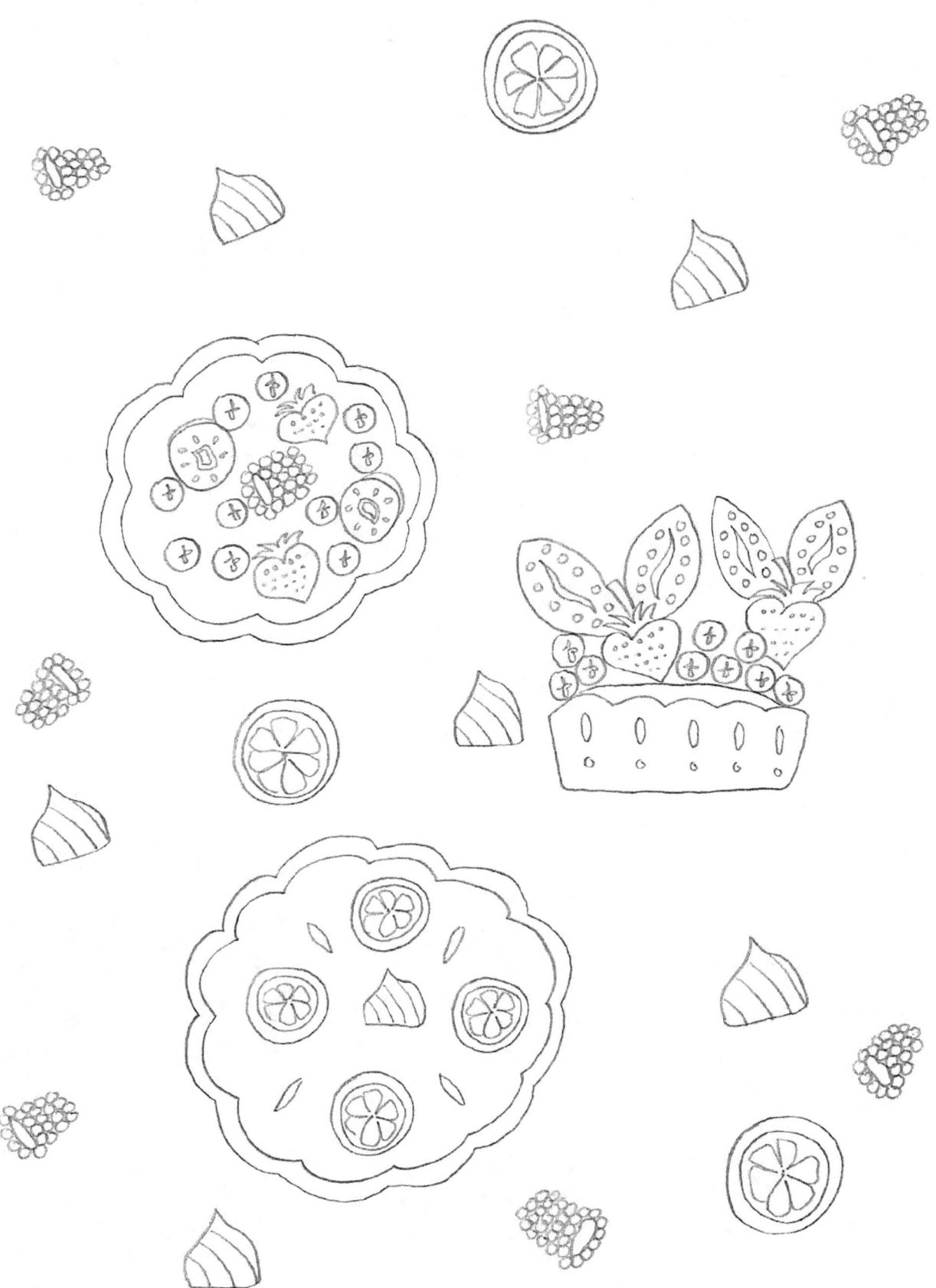

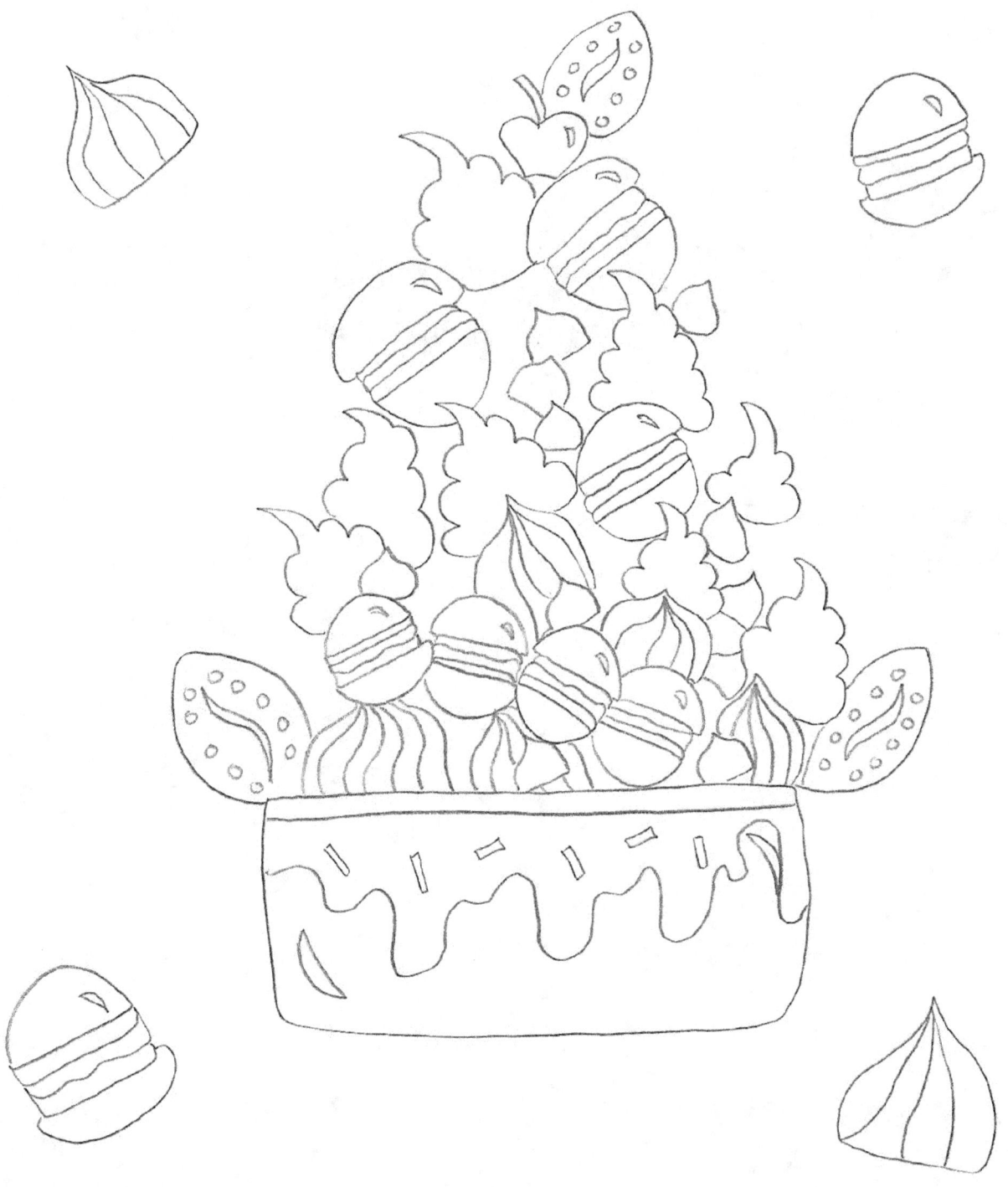

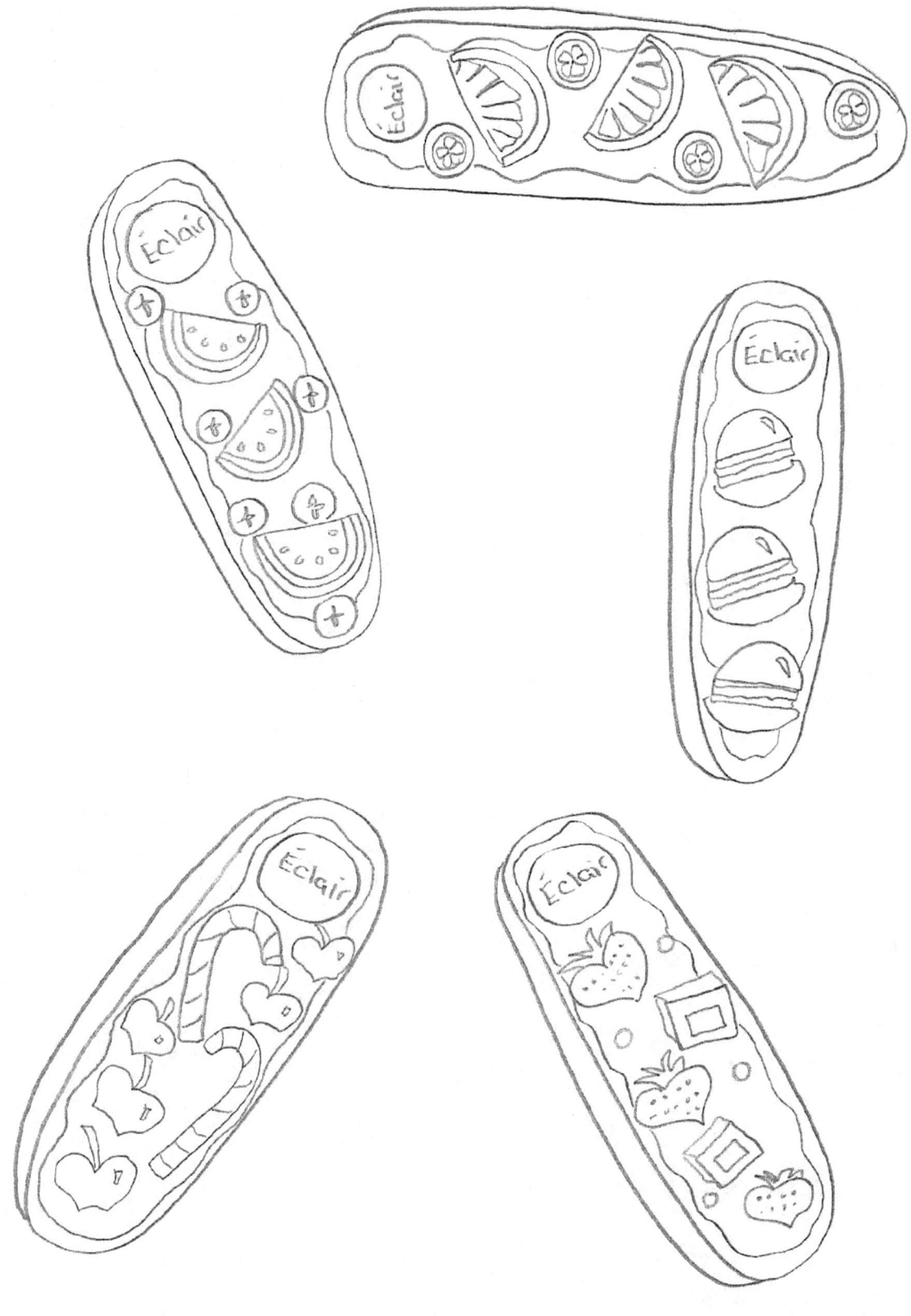

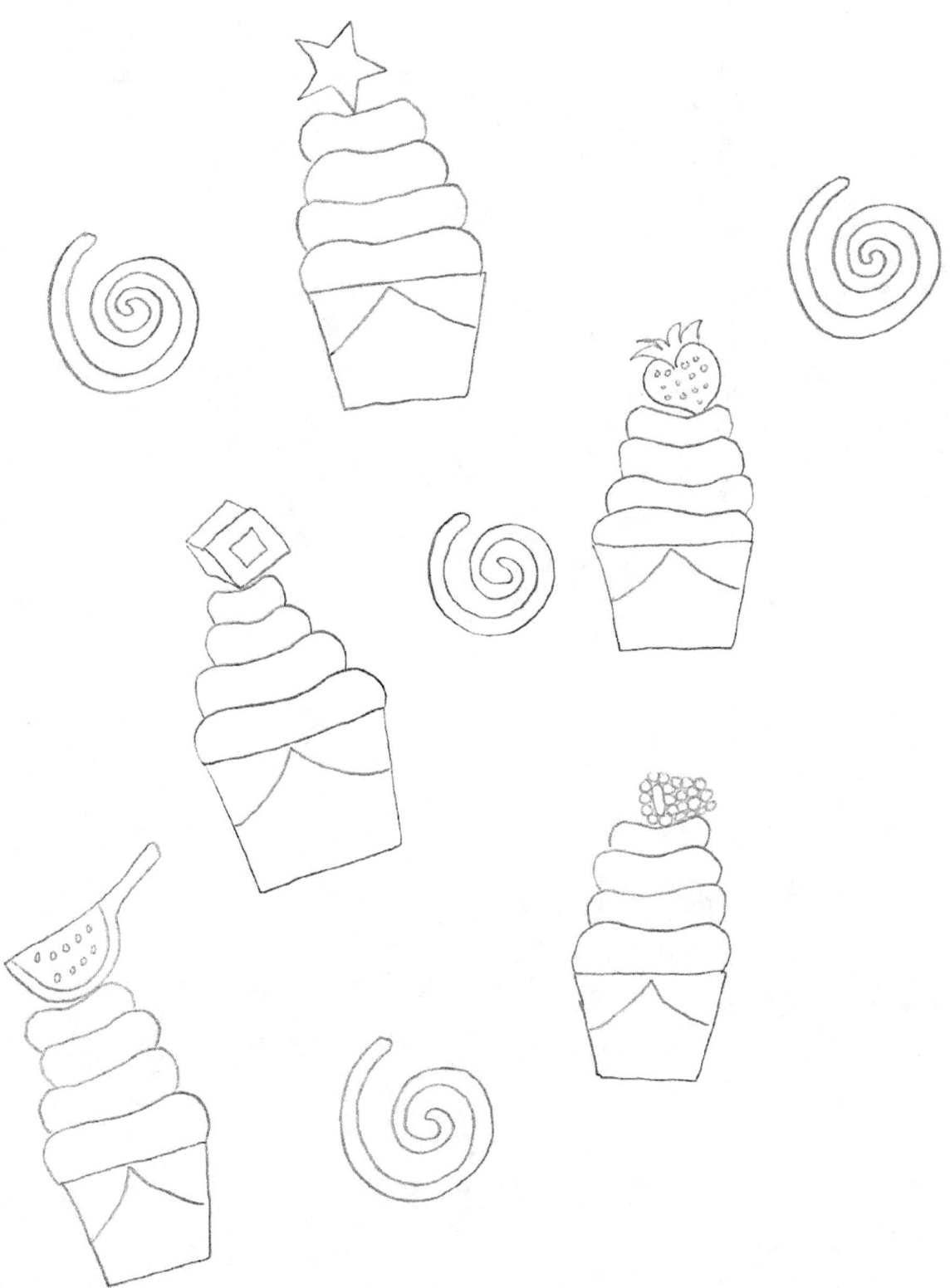

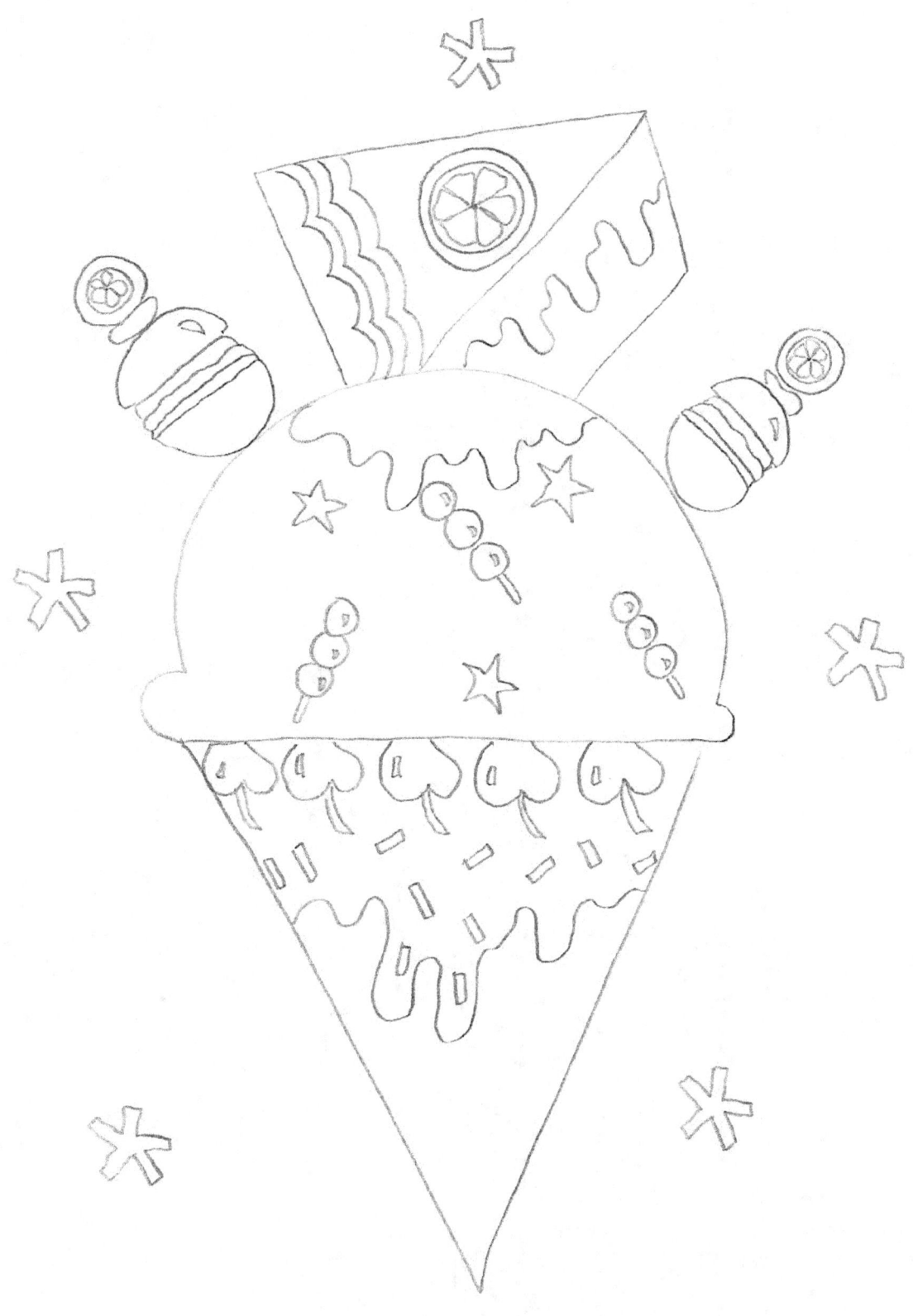

THANK YOU FOR PURCHASING MAGICAL DESSERTS COLORING BOOK. IF YOUR CHILD ENJOYED THEIR COLORING EXPERIENCE, YOU MIGHT FIND MY ADULT COLORING BOOKS INTERESTING FOR BOTH YOU AND YOUR CHILD. THE BELOW BOOKS CAN BE PURCHASED AT AMAZON.COM:

VINTAGE PARIS BAKE SHOP

ICE CREAM MADNESS

ICE CREAM MADNESS VOLUME 2

TEA & COFFEE TROPICAL TREASURES

TEA & COFFEE OCEAN TREASURES

TEA & COFFEE TREASURES

BOTANICAL FLOWERS & MANDALAS

MAJESTIC FALL

A VERY RETRO CHRISTMAS

A SPECIAL THANK YOU TO MY FRIEND, MARY ENGLES, WHO COLORED THE FRONT COVER.

IF YOU ENJOYED YOUR COLORING EXPERIENCE, PLEASE TELL OTHERS ABOUT IT BY WRITING A REVIEW ON AMAZON.COM UNDER THE BOOK YOU COLORED.

www.ingramcontent.com/pod-product-compliance
Lightning Source LLC
Chambersburg PA
CBHW081740220526
45468CB00008B/2176